ECUADOR vs. PERU

INTERNATIONAL PEACE ACADEMY
OCCASIONAL PAPER SERIES

ECUADOR vs. PERU

Peacemaking Amid Rivalry

Monica Herz
João Pontes Nogueira

LYNNE
RIENNER
PUBLISHERS

BOULDER
LONDON

Published in the United States of America in 2002 by
Lynne Rienner Publishers, Inc.
1800 30th Street, Boulder, Colorado 80301
www.rienner.com

and in the United Kingdom by
Lynne Rienner Publishers, Inc.
3 Henrietta Street, Covent Garden, London WC2E 8LU

Library of Congress Cataloging-in-Publication Data
Herz, Monica.
　　Ecuador vs. Peru : peacemaking amid rivalry / Monica Herz and Joao Pontes
Nogueira.
　　　　p. cm.—(International Peace Academy occasional paper series)
　　Includes bibliographical references and index.
　　ISBN 1-58826-075-5 (alk. paper)
　　1. Ecuador-Peru Conflict, 1995.　2. Ecuador—Foreign relations—Peru.
3. Peru—Foreign relations—Ecuador.　4. Peace treaties.　I. Title: Ecuador versus
Peru.　II. Nogueira, Joao Pontes.　III. Title.　IV. Series.
F3738.2.H479　2002
986.607'4—dc21

　　　　　　　　　　　　　　　　　　　　　　　　　　　　　2002017809

British Cataloguing in Publication Data
A Cataloguing in Publication record for this book
is available from the British Library.

Printed and bound in the United States of America

The paper used in this publication meets the requirements
of the American National Standard for Permanence of
Paper for Printed Library Materials Z39.48-1984.

5　4　3　2　1

Contents

Foreword

It is with great pleasure that we publish this IPA Occasional Paper detailing an important but little-known peace process that ended the enduring rivalry that has simmered between Ecuador and Peru for well over 100 years.

We are particularly delighted that the two authors, Monica Herz and João Pontes Nogueira, agreed to undertake this project in Brazil, where they both teach, traveling from there to carry out field research in Ecuador, Peru, and elsewhere. Brazil, notably President Henrique Cardoso, played an important part in coaxing the parties toward resolution of their bitter dispute.

This instance of peacemaking is interesting for several reasons. It did not involve mediation by the United Nations or the Organization of American States. Rather, negotiations were facilitated by four "guarantor" countries—Argentina, Brazil, Chile, and the United States—which had underwritten the earlier treaty between Ecuador and Peru that provided the framework for the ultimate settlement. Each brought particular attributes to the negotiating table. The private sector in both countries also played a very constructive role in urging their respective governments and parliaments to settle. As well, several important media organizations in each country forsook jingoistic coverage of the negotiations and attempted, with considerable success, to build mutual understanding.

Moreover, the agreement between Ecuador and Peru was reached at a time of considerable political instability in Ecuador, undercutting the belief in some academic circles that weak governments cannot make peace. Peru also was experiencing some domestic turmoil.

7

However, President Alberto Fujimori was consistently committed to a negotiated settlement, even falling out with some of his advisers over concessions they deemed excessive. It is remarkable, when visiting the two countries today, to note how widespread support for the agreement is. Even the militaries, initially quite reserved in both countries over the negotiating process, now appear to favor lasting peace.

More broadly, this case illustrates a disposition in Latin America to resolve disputes with the help of neighboring countries rather than multilateral institutions. Other continents have a lot to learn about the helpful role that neighbors can play, in the right circumstances, in the peacemaking process.

We are grateful to the Ford Foundation and the John D. and Catherine T. MacArthur Foundation for funding this project.

—David M. Malone
President, International Peace Academy

Acknowledgments

This research was made possible by the International Peace Academy's initiative to encourage the study of successful processes of peaceful conflict resolution in Latin America. We are particularly indebted to David Malone, who during a visit to Rio de Janeiro last year proposed the idea of writing an IPA Occasional Paper on the mediation process that led to the resolution of the Ecuador-Peru conflict. Integral funding for the research was provided by the IPA.

We would also like to acknowledge the support of the International Relations Institute of Pontifical Catholic University of Rio de Janeiro, where we both teach and conduct research. Grace Tanno was a valuable assistant during the initial stages of the project. We would like to thank Luciana Varanda for her utmost efficiency and patience in gathering crucial documentation and bibliographical information.

Special thanks are due to those who helped us in organizing the field trips to Peru and Ecuador. The Brazilian Embassy in Lima, especially Third Secretary Francisco Novello, made the arrangements and contacts without which important interviews would not have been possible. In Ecuador, Minister-Counselor Marcello Vasconcellos of the Brazilian Embassy in Quito organized our agenda and obtained interviews with central players in the conflict and negotiation process. Bertha Gallegos of the Catholic University of Ecuador organized our visit to Quito and was extremely kind in helping us to arrange interviews. Retired Colonel Francisco Molina, of the Ecuadorian army, was particularly helpful with contacts and interviews with members of the military who participated in the 1995 war.

Finally, we are grateful to the officials and specialists who generously gave up their time to receive us and who elucidated crucial aspects of the conflict and the negotiations. Their interviews are duly documented in the bibliography.

—Monica Herz
—João Pontes Nogueira

Ecuador-Peru Demilitarized Zone, 1995

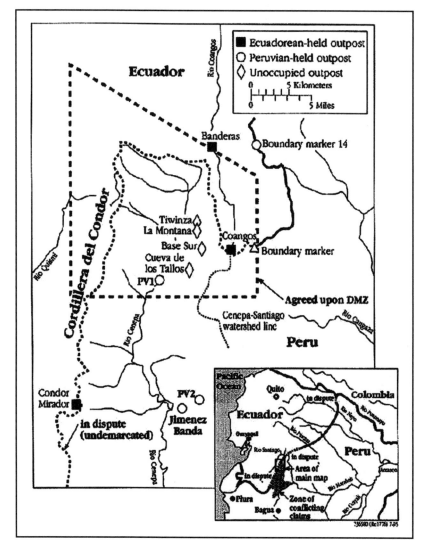

Source: Used with permission of the North-South Center Press and the School of International Studies, University of Miami. Originally published in the *Journal of Interamerican Studies and World Affairs* 39, no. 3 (1997): 120.

Note: Map is compiled from best available sources. The "in dispute" boundary line is an approximation of the undemarcated border between Ecuador and Peru that follows ridgelines of the Cordillera del Condor.

1

Introduction

In January 1995, the armies of Peru and Ecuador engaged in a confrontation in the region of the Cenepa valley, a remote location in the Amazon jungle, in what became a small-scale war that lasted thirty days. Both countries had been at war before over territorial issues. In 1941, Peru had defeated Ecuador in a brief conflict that consolidated territorial gains, particularly in the Amazon region, later recognized in the Rio de Janeiro Protocol of 1942.[1]

The 1995 war stands out as an interesting subject for study for a number of reasons, the foremost, perhaps, being that wars in South America became scarce in the twentieth century[2] and few observers believed one would occur in the more democratic and economically integrated post–Cold War Western Hemisphere. We will argue here that the outbreak of war can be explained within the context of a hostile relationship between the two countries concentrated around a territorial dispute with nineteenth-century origins. The rivalry between Peru and Ecuador had already produced several military exchanges over the past 100 years, one of which escalated into the small-scale war of 1941. However, more than the outbreak of the limited war in the Cenepa valley—which is the subject of Chapter 3—we are interested in the mechanisms of conflict management and resolution employed to prevent further escalation and bring the conflict to a close, and in how these mechanisms relate to the Latin American security environment.

We believe this otherwise relatively minor event is particularly interesting due to the involvement of three regional powers—Argentina, Brazil, Chile—and the United States in the mediation process that led to the negotiation of a peace settlement. The process, led by what the 1942 Rio Protocol defined as the *guarantor* countries, represents a successful instance of peaceful resolution of an old conflict, which had already produced two serious military confrontations and had the potential to involve both countries in a general war.

Another important aspect of the discussion developed here is the fact that the states in contention, as well as the third parties involved, negotiated the peace within the legal and institutional framework of the Rio Protocol, avoiding the participation of regional collective security organizations such as the Organization of American States (OAS) or other less institutional bodies such as the Rio Group. In fact, as we suggest at different points in our analysis, the choice of this ad hoc mechanism of conflict resolution may have brought the necessary flexibility to reach an agreement acceptable to all. The negotiated adjustment of the procedures stipulated by the Rio Protocol to the realities of the current crisis, which included a clearer definition of the role of the four guarantor countries, was crucial to the successful development of the mediation process. The principal aim of this research is an analysis of the conditions—domestic and international—that made the negotiations possible and of the dynamics of the process itself.

While our research is not aimed at discussing the validity of the democratic peace argument in the region, we do address the extent to which the preservation of a record of peacefulness and interstate stability determined the approach taken by the negotiators, particularly the guarantor countries, during the mediation process. We also consider the weight of economic factors in the actors' calculations, noting especially the negative impact of the war on both countries' economic reform policies, on the overall performance of the economy, and on their positions in the ongoing negotiations to form a free trade area in the Americas.

Although several sources interviewed by the authors mentioned the different approaches and positions taken by individual guarantor countries at various junctures of the three-year process, such differences are not treated here. Given the relatively recent conclusion of the Brasilia agreements and the nature and sources of the information needed, an objective investigation of the divergences among the guarantor countries in the negotiations would require separate research. Most officials interviewed for this work were reluctant to comment on the issue, stressing instead that occasional differences did not significantly influence the dynamics and final results of the process.[3] That point must remain moot. We believe our findings demonstrate that the most important aspect of the successful resolution of the conflict between Peru and Ecuador was the way in which the framework of the negotiating process structured the role of the group of guarantor countries and their relationship with the contending parties, and the way in which this framework allowed for changes in the attitudes of policymakers and public opinion in both countries.

Among the guarantors, certain personalities may have had a particularly central role in pushing the process forward and, at some critical junctures, in presenting alternatives that contributed to overcoming significant impasses: the names of President Fernando Henrique Cardoso of Brazil; Ambassador Luigi Einaudi, special representative for the United States; and Ambassador Ivan Canabrava, chief negotiator for Brazil, come to mind. However, as we are more concerned with the effectiveness of the mechanism of conflict resolution, we will look at the comprehensive role of the guarantors as a group in the context of the mediation process rather than concentrating on individual countries or personalities.

The analytical perspective adopted here, and discussed in more detail below, considers domestic variables in explaining the outcome of the negotiation and mediation processes. The participation of civil society organizations in the domestic debates that contributed to a gradual change in positions regarding the conflict in Ecuador, for instance, is an important factor in our analysis of the redefinition of interests and identities enabling an agreement. On the other hand, we will see how the internationalization of the process through the mediation mechanisms within the Rio Protocol contributed, in both countries, to insulate the influence of sectors resistant to an agreement within the military and foreign services. The negotiating framework also crucially insulated the process from the destabilizing pressures of serious domestic turmoil during the negotiating period, particularly in Ecuador.

We investigate the origins of the conflict, with special emphasis on the period that preceded the 1995 war, and analyze the mediation and negotiation processes that led to its resolution. We focus on the mechanisms that prevented the general escalation of the militarized dispute and produced a seemingly definitive settlement of what we have defined as an *enduring rivalry*.[4] In order to understand the trajectory that led to the rivalry we also examine the historical background of the territorial contention between Peru and Ecuador and the most important attempts to manage and resolve the conflict, either bilaterally or through mediation and arbitration.

The concept of rivalry is particularly helpful for the analysis of the relationship between Peru and Ecuador. While the immediate and structural causes of the wars of 1941 and 1995 are related to territorial disputes in several sectors of the border that can be traced back to the nineteenth century, the difficulties in settling these differences are due to the development of a pattern of rivalry between the two countries.

Gary Goertz and Paul Diehl have defined *rivalry* as a "relationship in which both sides deal with issues using the military tools of foreign policy and where militarized conflict between two states repeats itself." Since the competition between rival states is conducted militarily, there is a persistent expectation and risk of conflict. Hostility generated by past conflict is projected into future relations and, as the probability of war is increased, "peace" cannot be defined in this context merely by the absence of war but must depend on the condition of the rivalry. Goertz and Diehl categorize an enduring rivalry as lasting twenty to twenty-five years, during which five to seven conflicts occur; John Vasquez admits a less restrictive standard of at least two militarized disputes over a decade. In the case of Peru and Ecuador, hostility can be observed at least since the mid-nineteenth century, and there have been at least three armed conflicts in the past five decades. The hostility reflected in both countries' foreign policies did not oscillate sharply during that period, and the intensity of the 1941 war—taking casualties as a reference—was only marginally less than that of the 1995 Cenepa War, indicating that the rivalry did not follow an evolutionary pattern of escalation or de-escalation. However, commentators also note that the longer a rivalry persists, the greater the probability that it will end. Difficulties arise in determining the point in time at which the rivalry may legitimately be considered to have ended. While conventional security texts often attribute the closure of a dispute to the outcome of a war, war, in itself, is unlikely to end a rivalry. On the contrary, as a pattern of hostility is established, war fuels rivalry.

Commentators agree that the issue that sparks a rivalry is crucial to understanding it, and also that "territorial disputes are the main source of conflict that can give rise to a sequence of actions that ends in war."[5] Vasquez presents significant empirical evidence to show that dyads of rival contiguous states with territorial disputes account for the majority of interstate wars between 1816 and 1986. The territorial nature of the Peru-Ecuador rivalry helps to explain its endurance, the recurrent use of military force, and each party's resistance to negotiate a settlement.

Vasquez utilizes the dual concepts of a *stake dimension* and an *actor dimension* to highlight the combination of objective and subjective elements in the dynamics of rivalry.[6] In the Peru-Ecuador case, an intense hostility grounded in deep historical grievances suggests the development of an actor dimension that stymied several previous efforts at resolving the conflict. For Ecuador, not only was the claim to an outlet to the Amazon River Basin a central element of its national identity,[7] the existence of a permanent threat from Peru had substantively defined that country's international relations for the past five decades. For Peru and Ecuador, territoriality represented both an objective and a subjective interest—it had both a material value and a subjective value related to the essential characteristics of the state.

The pattern of interaction between the states—extreme competition and psychological hostility—goes beyond the "objective" consideration of the stakes from a rational, cost-benefit analysis.[8] Examining the *attitude* of states toward each other in explaining a conflict distances rivalry literature from *structural realist* perspectives.[9] In the conclusion to this study, we consider the possible ending of the Peru-Ecuador rivalry after the Brasilia Accords. If the Cenepa War is considered as one event in a long-standing rivalry, our analysis of the successful mediation of the territorial issue after the conflict may suggest directions for future research into the longer-term outcome of that relationship.

Our focus on interaction and relationship allows for the introduction of certain dimensions usually excluded from the study of conflicts. The absence of interdependence among countries has been noted by many analysts as a factor contributing to war; the approach taken here would suggest a rather high level of interdependence or "intimacy" in the process of reproduction of one another's identities through the dynamics of rivalry.

The resolution of the conflict through the negotiation process analyzed in this work necessarily involves the redefinition of interests and identities by both sides, in an effort that takes place both at the unit level and at the interaction level. We must look, then, both to the domestic and the external realms to explain the changes in attitude that made the agreements possible. We explore the domestic economic and political conditions that contribute to redefining the national interest, and the difficult and often dramatic dialogue taking place at the negotiation table. For Goertz and Diehl, "domestic political factors and issue salience seem to be most associated with rivalry termination."[10] Issues such as liberalization and the relevance of territoriality in the contemporary international context become relevant here.

While we describe and analyze the negotiation process and the conditions in which it takes place, we also emphasize the mediation of the guarantor countries as essential to the outcome. According to Goertz and Diehl, rivalries are seldom affected by mediation except, perhaps, in delaying the outbreak of the next conflict. Why was mediation accepted by both sides in 1995? This is a question we examine at some length.

We explore the cultural and ideational factors that contribute to the regional security environment at the time of the conflict. We highlight relevant norms and values that characterize the particular Latin American context in the 1990s and consider the role they play in reshaping state identities and interests. We argue that the "culture" of the Latin American regional system is consistent with the existence of rivalries such as that investigated here, at the same time as it constrains the actors to recognize sovereignty rights, refrain from expansionism, and make efforts to legitimize the resolution of territorial disputes through international law.[11] Sovereignty is the central institution of this type of system and is protected by international law. But, as rivals, states are uncertain about the balance of threat and may choose to use force to secure their sovereignty. In this relatively stable environment, wars are motivated by issues such as territory and strategic advantage rather than the destruction and conquest of other states. We believe this characterization of the "culture of anarchy" in Latin America may promote an understanding of the way in which Peru and Ecuador sustained an enduring rivalry under a regional order that sought the consolidation of peaceful means of conflict resolution through international institutions, but also tolerated, without any significant collective action, recurrent militarized disputes. The ending of this enduring rivalry may be an indication that the Latin American culture of anarchy is changing in the wake of momentous global transformations.

In the following chapters we discuss the historical background of the rivalry between Peru and Ecuador (Chapter 2), the conditions that led to the outbreak of the 1995 Cenepa War (Chapter 3); and the mediation process that led to the definitive resolution of the conflict (Chapter 4). In the conclusion we briefly discuss the significance of this process to the Latin American security context, indicate elements supporting the argument that the rivalry has been terminated, and evaluate the experience in the light of current concerns about the institutionalization of conflict resolution mechanisms in the hemisphere.

NOTES

1. The 1942 Rio Protocol of Peace, Friendship and Boundaries was signed between Peru and Ecuador after the war of 1941, in which Peru defeated Ecuador and occupied portions of its territory. The historical precedents and the significance of the protocol are discussed in Chapter 2.

2. Kalevi J. Holsti, *The State, War and the State of War* (Cambridge: Cambridge University Press, 1996).

3. The former minister of Foreign Relations of Brazil, Ambassador Luis Felipe Lampreia, expressed this view quite emphatically.

4. Gary Goertz and Paul Diehl, "Enduring Rivalries: Theoretical Constructs and Empirical Patterns," *International Studies Quarterly* 37 (1995); John Vasquez, "Distinguishing Rivals That Go to War from Those That Do Not . . . ," *International Studies Quarterly* 40 (1996).

5. Vasquez, "Dinstinguishing Rivals," p. 535.

6. Ibid., p. 532.

7. We borrow here Alexander Wendt's definition of identity as "a property of intentional actors that generates motivational and behavioral dispositions," and his consideration of identities being constituted by "internal and external structures." Alexander Wendt, *Social Theory of International Politics* (Cambridge: Cambridge University Press, 1999).

8. John Vasquez, "Reexamining the Steps to War: New Evidence and Theoretical Insights," *Handbook of War Studies II* (Ann Arbor: University of Michigan Press, 1999).

9. Structural realism is concerned with the occurrence of war in anarchic systems where the distribution of power capabilities defines structures that are more or less permissive to conflict. The structural perspective is mainly positional; interactions are not relevant to the analysis because they are attributes of the units. Rivalry literature focuses on the interaction and relationships of states in order to explain conflict because the positional pic-

ture does not explain why relations among some states develop into conflict and others don't, or why a certain behavior can be perceived either as a threat or as a benign gesture.

10. Goertz and Diehl, "Enduring Rivalries."

11. Wendt, *Social Theory*, p. 249.

2

Conflict and Mediation
in Historical Perspective

The 1995 Cenepa War was perhaps the last episode in a long territorial dispute between Peru and Ecuador that began, according to many analysts, at the time these countries reached their independence in the early decades of the nineteenth century.[1] The length, the recurrence of armed confrontations, the issue at stake, and the hostility that characterize this relationship allow us to define it as an *enduring rivalry*.[2] In this chapter we will look at the rivalry's historical record in an attempt to explain why a territorial dispute—a common problem in nineteenth-century South America—became the central issue in these countries' often hostile relationship over the course of a century. The structure of Peru and Ecuador's interaction in the international system was built around the historical grievances over their undefined border, and their identities as states were defined in good measure by their rivalry.

The first section of this chapter addresses the centrality of the *sovereign territorial ideal* in the nineteenth-century process of South American republic building.[3] While the statistical data presented by Vasquez demonstrate that territory is the principal issue fueling rivalries that escalate into war, we also emphasize the important role territory has had in the consolidation of sovereignty in the history of the region. We next examine the importance of the *open border* to the construction of national identity. The conflicts that distinguished their rivalry had an impact upon the domestic political stability of both Peru and Ecuador. At times they increased the risk of fragmentation of then weak states; in other instances, they mobilized society in defense of the state and strengthened it. One of the characteristics of enduring rivalries is the considerable difficulty in establishing

21

negotiations over the issue in contention, the likelihood of failure, and the negative effects of frustrated efforts on the level of hostility, which can lead to the use of force. In the third section we investigate some of the more significant attempts at mediation and the more serious crises occurring before the 1941 war.

Finally, we discuss the causes of the war and the historical context in which the Rio Protocol was signed. This last section is particularly important because one of the crucial problems regarding the rivalry during the second half of the twentieth century was the parties' recognition, interpretation, and implementation of the protocol. In fact, the Cenepa War may best be understood in the light of the 1942 Rio Protocol and the events and processes that produced and followed its conclusion. The protocol is a landmark for our analysis of the recent war because it represents both the high point of collective and bilateral efforts to end the dispute before the 1998 Brasilia Accords and the element of discord around which the conflicting claims are stated. The protocol also embodies the first successful international mediation by regional powers and the United States to end the conflict, and the instrument that would be reactivated to bring the 1995 crisis, not to mention the oldest territorial dispute in the subcontinent and probably the rivalry itself, to a definite end.

TERRITORY AND STATE BUILDING

The process by which European colonial possessions in the Americas became independent constitutes an extraordinary experience of state building in the modern history of international relations. The new states were formed in a struggle against the forces of old empires, under the influence of new liberal republican ideas and facing the daunting challenge of unifying vast, and often unknown, land masses, with scarce material and institutional resources.[4] The difficulties that faced the new states related not only to the occupation, definition, administration, and defense of their territories. The political task was all the more complex because the very principle of sovereign territoriality, as it is understood in its modern formulation, was not in Europe itself consolidated in state practice. In fact, the link between sovereignty and territoriality would be strengthened in the eighteenth century when "a functional order based on separate territorial structures made territory an ever more significant base for power."[5] This link was reinforced during the second half of the century by the growing influences of nationalism, an ideology based on the identification of a people (a nation) with territory.[6]

Territory came to be interpreted as an essential element for the organization of national power as well as a systemic principle that secured the stability of international relations and the integrity of sovereign states. Despite constant challenges to the territorial integrity of states by expansionist policies within and without Europe, the ideal consolidated itself and became, in Murphy's words, "the only imaginable spatial framework for political life."[7]

The South American republics had to come to terms with their new condition in a context in which the basic organizing principles of the modern international system were still contested. Their process of decolonization did not occur at a time when the notion of self-determination was legitimized in any legal instrument of international law, as happened with the decolonization of European colonies after World War II or even the constitution of independent states after the fall of the Habsburg, Romanov, and Ottoman Empires. The elites who led the struggle for independence and the efforts to build new states had to agree on a principle that would allow for the constitution of independent units and build a regional system that would not be bent on territorial revisionism, especially after the more ambitious designs of Ibero-American unity failed and gave way to the fragmentation of the colonial administrative units. Simon Bolivar's dream faded in the harsh light of divided oligarchies possessing scant notions of what could unite postcolonial communities, except, perhaps, the protection of their land and privileges, and the exclusion of the Indian and Mestizo majorities from power. The result was the formation of weak states that lacked legitimacy, that could boast only a level of integration that allowed for centralized administrative control of the territory, and, crucially, that were marked by contested boundaries.[8] In fact, the cohesion of these states was constantly threatened for most of the nineteenth century by foreign intervention and wars over territory, by regional strife with strong centrifugal tendencies, and by chronic internal political instability.

However, as we have suggested, the weakness of the South American republics was aggravated by the frailty of the sovereign territorial ideal in the international system itself. During the first half of the century, Europe experienced what Eric Hobsbawm defined as the *Age of Revolution,* when hardly any country escaped periods of upheaval that threatened the future and integrity of liberal nation states. The problem was to establish an organizing principle around which new, weak, and insecure states would converge.

The legal instrument adopted to establish the limits of the new republics was that of *uti possedetis*, which recognized the boundaries of the administrative units of the Spanish colonial empire as the basis for their territorial claims. The principle was recognized by most countries at the 1826 Congress of Panama and later at the 1848 Lima Conference, and aimed to provide basic guarantees that the boundaries of the new states would be legally secured as successors of the colonial territories, regardless of their capability effectively to occupy those areas. This formulation became also known as *uti possedetis de jure*, and was applied to the decolonization process in Africa as well, producing what Robert Jackson has called *negative sovereignty*, the legal entitlement to rule a territory without the material and institutional capabilities to exercise that right.[9]

The South American effort to develop rules to govern the formation of a regional system of states that aspired to become fully recognized in the international stage expressed an early concern about the role international law could play in the prevention of expansionism and foreign aggression. Interestingly, the central place of territoriality in the system may account for the comparative stability of its boundaries and the low incidence of wars in the past 100 years—despite the occurrence of several interstate wars during the nineteenth century—especially when considered against the dismal record of territorial revisionism and catastrophic interstate wars in Europe during the same period. The principle of *uti possedetis de jure* had, however, considerable shortcomings given its potential to clash with principles and patterns of nation building associated with the rise of late nineteenth-century nationalism, especially the claim to the right of self-determination. As we will see, the old doctrine was often ignored in favor of geopolitical imperatives perceived by nationalist elites as crucial to consolidate the state.

Territoriality plays, then, a central role in the construction of the national identities of most Latin American states, and their histories are often written through the cartographic illustration of their struggles to conquer the space where the *imagined community* can realize its aspiration to independence and freedom.[10] For example, the cartographic discourse that is so important in the teaching of history in Ecuadorian schools becomes a central tool in the "making of the nation" and in the construction of the civic idea of "Ecuadorian-ness."[11] The history of the country is told by and through representations of its territorial dispossession. In the case of Peru, the defeat in the War of the Pacific and the consequent loss of significant portions of territories in its southern provinces to Chile represent a traumatic experience that threatens the integrity of the nation but also contributes to the emergence of a new conceptualization of Peruvian identity.[12]

Ecuador "is defined as being a nation that has lost territory": the conflict with Peru and the image of the open border, which was later characterized as the "open wound," becomes instrumental in the establishment of national identity.[13] The very coincidence of Ecuador's name with the line of the equator contributed to an association of the discourse of nationality with the spatial representations of the new science of geography, which became a fundamental tool of state and empire building during the nineteenth and early twentieth centuries. Indeed, the existence of these states—their sovereignty and their national identity—is intimately related to the establishment of their territory and its protection by stable boundaries. As we will see in the following section, territorial conflict keeps the border open and defers the constitution of the nation, whose existence and future as a bounded community become tied to the dynamics of its rivalry toward the "other." The "closure" of the process of state building can, from this perspective, be linked and analyzed concomitantly with the process leading to the end of the enduring rivalry.

THE OPEN BORDER

Ever since Peru and Ecuador gained independence, the delimitation of their boundaries has been the object of dispute. Peru became an independent state in the aftermath of the battle of Ayacucho (1824), and Ecuador seceded from Gran Colombia in 1830. The first negotiations and conflicts over the border—including the Treaty of Guayaquil (1829)—took place between Peru and Gran Colombia. The application of the doctrine of *uti possedetis de jure* would suggest that Peru's and Ecuador's origins as political entities derive from the history of, respectively, the viceroyalty of Peru and the *audiencia* de Quito.

The adoption of *uti possedetis* did not prevent clashes between the two countries over the demarcation of their frontiers. In fact, the boundaries of the colonial territories were so irregular that the application of the doctrine created a whole new set of arguments about, for instance, the interpretation of colonial decrees, the origins of the expedition that discovered the source of the Amazon River, and other historical issues that reinforced the claims of one side or the other. Indeed, an increasing reliance on a mass of historical arguments that frequently cited events in the distant past of each nation probably served to crystallize both sides' positions and create additional difficulties in reaching an agreement. The rivalry developed through the powerful mechanism of projecting the hostile relationship through past claims over the disputed area, reinforcing the perception that the identities of each nation were formed in and through an exclusionary and conflictual relationship over the centuries.

Ecuador, for instance, contested Peruvian arguments about the interpretation and relevance of a royal decree of 1802 (Cédula Real), which transferred the responsibility for the occupation and evangelization of the provinces of Maynas and Quijos from the *audiencia* of Quito to the viceroyalty of Peru as the basis for claims to that territory.[14] Ecuador insisted that the Cédula Real did not confer political rights upon Peru and that consequently *uti possedetis de jure* did not apply. It also argued that the Inca prince Athaualpa's victory over his brother from Cuzco in the sixteenth century established the supremacy of Quito over the region.[15]

Clearly, *uti possedetis* was useful in many instances of state building in South America, but, as in the case of Peru and Ecuador, several political issues could not be resolved merely by its application. The principle was thus gradually reinterpreted by the Peruvians as meaning the de facto occupation of the territory as the basis for sovereignty claims, even before the 1848 Lima Conference. Perhaps the most evident difficulty in supporting the de jure interpretation of the doctrine concerned Peru's effective and progressive occupation of the Amazon Basin, mainly from Iquitos, in a colonization effort that Ecuador could not match, either due to geographical disadvantages in gaining access to the region or because it simply lacked the resources and the drive to occupy the territory it claimed. In this sense, the Peruvian advance to and beyond the Marañon's northern shores was apparently a gradual process that reflected the fact that the border remained open not only because there was no agreement about where it should be demarcated but also because the legal instrument that accorded sovereignty without occupation was particularly ineffective in the depths of the mostly unexplored Amazon frontier. Since the border remained open for so long and along extensive tracts of territory, it became more "flexible" and subject to a wide array of interpretations. The disparities among the lines traced, from that defined by the Pedemonte-Mosquera Protocol of 1830 (the validity of which is contested by Peru) to that established by the Rio Protocol of 1942 and including several other proposed lines, are remarkable.[16]

Self-determination was another significant principle recognized in South America, allowing for the secession of Bolivia from Peru and of Ecuador from Gran Colombia. While it was not applied indiscriminately, self-determination often clashed with claims based on ownership, as in the case of Peru's loss of territory now part of Bolivia. Such territorial shifts created considerable resentment among those who suffered disproportionate losses, such as Peru and Ecuador, feelings that constantly fueled animosity toward neighbors.

Resolution of Peruvian-Ecuadorian border problems during the nineteenth century was made particularly difficult by the weakness of both states. The open border increasingly became a sign of weakness, perhaps spurring increased efforts to address the issue in the final quarter of the century, when developments at the domestic and international levels posed new challenges to the cohesion of both nations. The Creole elite, supported by the military, had ruled Peru since independence, marginalizing the majority indigenous Indian population. The idea of a nation was, for a long period, nothing more than the preservation of the property and privileges of the landed oligarchies.[17] The first wave of nationalist movements with a more inclusive and less militaristic agenda emerged only after Peru's defeat in the Pacific War (1879–1883). The strength of the so-called civilizing movement in Peru abetted new efforts toward the resolution of the dispute with Ecuador, as did the fear that the Ecuadorian problem would weaken Peru's position if a new conflict with Chile emerged. Ecuador was a country similarly ravaged by political instability, lack of territorial integration, and civil wars during its first several decades as an independent nation.

In 1859–1860, a war broke out, apparently because of Peru's reaction to Ecuador's attempt to exchange contested territory for credits owed to England. A civil war erupted in Ecuador as a result of the Peruvian invasion, effectively dividing the country among regional forces, and Guayaquil was again occupied by Peru, the first occupation having occurred in 1829. Thanks to the alliance with one of the factions in the war, Peru obtained recognition of claims based on a 1802 royal decree. The 1860 Treaty of Mapasingue, which ended the war, was later denounced by both congresses. This somber episode in Ecuadorian history, which almost caused the country's fragmentation, is an interesting example of the effects of the open border: a blurring of boundaries (and identities) between the political forces involved in the conflict that was both international and internal. Efforts to negotiate the closure of the border in the ensuing decades can be interpreted as a response to the extreme instability of the previous period. Paradoxically, the rivalry develops and becomes enduring in the period when negotiations are attempted with greater resolve.

It was only by the late 1880s and early 1890s that both countries reached some degree of national integration and governmental stability that allowed for more concrete negotiations to take place on border issues. Until then, territorial issues, although of concern, were deferred to some point in the future. All of the several Ecuadorian constitutions drafted during the nineteenth century contained an article with a formula that recognized the current boundaries "until an agreement with the neighbor countries was concluded." It is interesting that Ecuador's most important legal document, in its various historical forms, did not contain a clear affirmation of Ecuador's territorial claims but rather deferred the definition of its borders to future international negotiations. International recognition seems to be as important as internal legitimization and integration in Latin American state-building processes. That may be the reason for the constant presence, from the early days of independence and the first border conflicts, of some sort of international arbitration or mediation.

CONFLICT AND ATTEMPTS AT MEDIATION

Enduring rivalries register a considerably higher incidence of attempts by third parties or multilateral organizations to manage conflict and mediate efforts toward resolution. Direct negotiation can be difficult to initiate and to conduct, given the high levels of hostility and the lack of trust that characterize this type of relationship. Consequently, there are incentives for the recourse to external mediation, even though its effectiveness can often be undermined by the involved parties' resistance to proposals perceived as concessions over an issue around which positions have crystallized.[18] Compared to other rivalries and conflicts, "the expected number of mediation attempts for enduring rivalries is ten times greater," and, as noted above, territorial rivalries are more likely to become enduring.[19] The rivalry examined here presents a type of recurring conflict of variable intensity that escalated twice into war and was the object of international attention for most of its duration, although with considerable oscillations, reflecting external, bilateral, and domestic conditions.

As early as 1827, Peru requested mediation by the United States in the matter of its border with what was then Gran Colombia. Although by the time the U.S. government responded positively an alternative agreement had been reached, it is significant that third-party involvement was considered at this historical juncture.[20] The most important instance of international involvement before the Rio Protocol was the Spanish arbitration requested by both countries in 1887, through the Espinoza-Bonifaz Protocol. This was, perhaps, the first serious attempt at establishing diplomatic negotiations aiming at conflict resolution. At the time, both countries had experienced serious domestic crises that threatened the ruling elite's hold on power and increased the cost of external instability generated by growing tensions at the border. Ecuador was still recovering from the turmoil of the 1860 civil war, and, in 1884, Peru had just suffered a major defeat in the Pacific War. The parties agreed to submit their differences to the arbitration of the Spanish crown, but the procedures established by the convention were too vague to generate the confidence necessary for the acceptance of an eventual solution.[21] There were still, however, favorable conditions domestically—and the vulnerability concerns mentioned above—encouraging some form of negotiation.

As a result of bilateral efforts, Peru and Ecuador signed the Herrera-Garcia Treaty, which, in retrospect, was perhaps the one proposal in the entire history of the rivalry that came closest to satisfying Ecuador's claims. It established a sovereign access to the Marañon River, and thus to the Amazon Basin, through the cession by Peru of significant areas of the disputed territory. The Ecuadorian

Congress approved the treaty in 1890, but the Peruvian legislature made amendments later refused by Ecuador, and the agreement became moot in 1894.[22] The vulnerability caused by defeat in the War of the Pacific, which initially functioned as an incentive to negotiate, may have increased the domestic sensibility regarding territorial concessions to another—weaker—neighbor. On the other hand, the conditions imposed by the Peruvian Congress did not affect the essence of the agreement, which granted Ecuador's central claim to a sovereign access to the Marañon River.

The enduring rivalry's *actor dimension,* which, according to Vasquez, displaces the focus from consideration of the stakes to the psychological relationship and hostility toward the other actor, may explain the reasons for this missed opportunity. Ecuador has been criticized for its insistence, on this occasion, on "maximalist" claims. The enduring rivalry approach provides a more sophisticated explanation for the failure of the treaty. Instead of placing too much emphasis on the apparently "irrational" behavior of the actors, it focuses on the dynamics of the interaction and the subjective and objective nature of the issue at stake.

Once bilateral efforts had exhausted their potential for conflict resolution, the parties decided to revive the Spanish Arbitration in 1904, in the midst of renewed military incidents at the border that threatened to escalate. According to Marcel Biato, Peruvian occupation of the Amazon Basin intensified with the rubber extraction boom at the beginning of the twentieth century under the auspices of the state and, when necessary, with military support.[23] The arbitration process lagged until 1910 when, on the eve of the king's opinion being declared, Ecuador decided not to accept the decision because information had leaked that it would favor Peru. The award in fact proposed a line of demarcation very close to the Peruvian conditions to the *Herrera-Garcia Treaty*, securing Ecuador's sovereign access to the Amazon Basin but confirming Peru's considerable territorial gains achieved by the occupation of the oriental area north of Iquitos up to the border with Colombia. With hindsight it can be argued, as Bruce St. John has done, that the Ecuadorian rejection of the award was a mistake because it conferred more territory than the country would ever receive in the settlements of 1941 and 1998. The failure of another negotiation that could have settled the dispute along reasonable lines exemplifies the difficulties posed by the dynamics of rivalry when the issue at hand is control over territory, especially when the fragility of the states involved increases the threat offered by the open border to the formation and consolidation of national identity.

The breakdown of negotiations that culminated in Ecuador's rejection of the Spanish Arbitration produced a steady escalation of tensions that almost led to war. This time, mediation by Argentina, Brazil, and the United States was accepted and played an important part in defusing the situation. However, the mediators did not succeed in convincing the parties to accept an arbitration. Ecuador was suspicious of any arbitration processes similar to the previous Spanish initiative and favored a different framework that would allow more space for direct negotiations. The Ponce-Castro Oyanguren Protocol of 1924 reflected that preference but failed in producing any significant progress before another round of negotiations took place, this time in Washington, D.C., at a conference held between 1936 and 1938 when political conditions were less favorable—another serious military incident had occurred at the border in 1936. Peru had already engaged in a military buildup that would give it the strategic edge later evident in the war of 1941.

The Washington Conference was a protracted exercise in diplomatic patience and was largely unproductive. In fact, its failure reinforced antagonism between the parties and the perception that a peaceful resolution of the dispute was nowhere in sight. Even though both sides accepted the possibility of a final comprehensive arbitration by the United States, the approaches to the territorial issue were even more distant than in the previous decades. The pattern that would characterize positions during the decades that followed 1942 had already emerged: Ecuador insisted on an extensive negotiation over the sovereignty of the provinces north of the Marañon River based on its legal claims (and the doctrine of *uti possedetis de jure),* while Peru insisted on restricting the discussion to the demarcation of de facto occupied territory. The necessary combination of legal and political formulas couldn't be achieved within the negotiating framework of the Washington Conference. Moreover, it became increasingly clear that the international mediation of the most powerful states in the Americas was unable to produce an acceptable agreement; this perception validated strategies of self-help that would ultimately lead to military escalation.

By 1938–1939 the attention of the United States and of the rest of the continent was focused on events in Europe and in the Pacific.

Given the stakes at hand and in the context of the threat of global war, the incentives increased to use force in a localized and swift operation. That was probably Peru's calculation in 1941. Besides, the Ecuadorian position had been progressively weakened after the failure of the Spanish Arbitration because its rejection of the final decision was regarded internationally as undermining a long process that had been agreed on by the two parties years before. In addition, the protraction of the dispute had not only increased the distance between the positions of the parties but also created opportunities for advance and consolidation of the Peruvian occupation of the region. With the failure of the negotiations in Washington, the situation remained precariously stabilized along the so-called status quo line recognized by the Act of Lima (1936), which basically maintained the boundary according to the positions held by each side but without recognition of territorial rights.[24]

THE RIO DE JANEIRO PROTOCOL

As we have seen briefly in the previous section, the border conflict between Peru and Ecuador may be interpreted as a particular aspect of the long and conflict-ridden historical process of nation building typical of South American republics. The unsettled border may be viewed as an expression of the travails of constituting a national identity and articulating it territorially. On the other hand, the historical record shows that the issue has been since its inception a subject of international interest, mediation, and, occasionally, intervention. More often than not, third-party involvement produced disappointing results and may have heightened tensions by creating expectations and frustrating the parties' hopes of a peaceful settlement, thus increasing the opportunity costs of the use of force. In fact, the use of force appears in Latin American history as a frequent alternative in border disputes, especially in the nineteenth century, given the difficulty of implementing the *uti possedetis* doctrine due, in part, to the lack of precise demarcation of colonial frontiers, in part to diverging interpretations of the doctrine itself. Brazil, for instance, favored a de facto interpretation that meant effective occupation was a determining factor in settling a dispute when legal boundaries were unclear: a view that could legitimize the use of force. Most of the skirmishes between Ecuador and Peru along the border can be explained by this rationale: military presence meant *effective occupation*. According to Calvert, "it was therefore possible—and indeed desirable—to establish a military presence as rapidly as possible in disputed frontier regions, which could in subsequent negotiations be used as evidence of effective occupation."[25] The 1942 Rio de Janeiro Protocol in many respects confirmed the actual practice of the major South American states, who saw too many contradictions and shortcomings in defining their national space on the basis of colonial titles.

Military solutions were insufficient to bring closure to the issue during the nineteenth century. Peru had always been superior before an often unprepared and weak Ecuadorian army. Although military strength contributed to consolidating Peruvian control of areas in the Amazon region it had already been occupying, no major armed conflict took place that could grant strategic victory. A pattern emerged of the kind usually found in enduring rivalries: military incidents are fairly frequent, becoming part of the relationship but not an efficient means of ending the rivalry itself. However, rivalry literature stresses the likelihood of militarized disputes escalating into war when territory is the central issue in contention. The failure of international mediation and arbitration; the difficulties in reestablishing bilateral negotiations that had previously produced little results; and the growing perception that the situation on the ground was deteriorating, with increasing numbers of troops from both sides trying to occupy sectors of the disputed border, created the conditions for the outbreak of the war of 1941.

Alleging Ecuadorian violations of the line of status quo, a reinforced Peruvian army achieved a swift victory at several points along the border, and occupied the provinces of El Oro and Loja, inside Ecuadorian territory, in July 1941. Although President Manuel Prado of Peru at first preferred a diplomatic solution, the influence of the army's commander, General Eloy Ureta, was crucial to the decision to attack: he threatened the government with a military coup if not authorized to advance over Tumbez.[26] Clashes began in July and overwhelmed the Ecuadorian army—weakened by fears of political uprising in Quito that forced President Arroyo del Rio to retain contingents to protect the government—in a little less than three months' time, producing a limited number of casualties.[27] The results of this Peruvian victory were quite significant. First, it established Peru's strategic superiority on the ground, demonstrating that country's will to engage in war in order to consolidate its positions within the disputed area and force Ecuador into an agreement to demarcate the border. Second, it prompted an international reaction that proved more effective than all previous attempts at mediation, given the hemispheric security concerns at the time. The United States, Brazil, and Argentina took immediate steps to broker an armistice by the beginning of October 1941. A month later, military observers from those three countries were present at the sites where hostilities had taken place, to monitor the agreement and to negotiate the establishment of a demilitarized zone agreed to by the parties.[28]

These two factors combined seem to have contributed decisively to the celebration of the Rio Protocol only six months after the conflict. Peru's strategic victory encouraged Ecuador to seek a quick settlement, fearing further deterioration in its position. The war in Europe and the outbreak of the war in the Pacific in December 1941 generated systemic pressures toward the pacification of the continent in the face of an increasingly unstable international environment. Indeed the protocol was signed, on January 29, 1942, at the conclusion of the third Consultative Meeting of the Foreign Affairs Ministers of the American States, convened to discuss the continent's coordinated response to the now concrete threat from the Axis powers. The negotiations were conducted at the margins of the conference, under considerable pressure, particularly from the United States and Brazil, to reach a quick agreement. The proceedings of the meeting do not even mention the war between Peru and Ecuador, except in the speech of Brazilian foreign minister Oswaldo Aranha at its closure.

The protocol essentially confirmed the 1936 line of status quo as the basis for the definitive boundary between the two countries, meaning that Ecuador would not obtain the access to the Marañon and Amazon Rivers that it had claimed since the nineteenth century, and would definitively surrender any claim to the vast territories in the Amazon Basin—the *Oriente*—on the basis of historical and legal rights that had been reaffirmed during the previous 100 years. For the most bitter critics of the protocol, Ecuador was deprived by signing of 40 percent of its territory. This figure, however, reflects maximalist claims (based on the Pedemonte-Mosquera Protocol of 1830), which in 1942 were unrealistic. If the Herrera-Garcia Treaty is taken as a reference point, Ecuador's territorial losses appear much lighter. In any case, the defeat was humiliating, and the terms of the peace did little to help Ecuador recover its dignity. The protocol became, in

Ecuador, a symbol of injustice and incomprehension by powerful hemispheric states of the legitimate claims of one of the smaller members of the "American family of states." In Peru, meanwhile, mediation by the guarantor countries was resented because it denied Peru's right to negotiate peace terms from the position of superiority gained by its military prowess.

Despite negative public opinion, especially in Ecuador, the settlement was finally approved by both legislative bodies shortly after its signature. After considerable difficulties emerged during the process of demarcating the actual border, the parties asked Brazil to arbitrate, within the framework of the protocol, differences regarding eight separate locations in the western and eastern sectors. The Aranha Formula of 1944, named after the Brazilian foreign minister, was a first and, with hindsight, crucial effort by Brazil to resolve issues regarding the implementation of the protocol. The formula was accepted by the other guarantor countries as well as by the parties. It led to arbitration, technically conducted by the Brazilian navy officer Braz Diaz de Aguiar in 1945. The formula solved most of the disputes, but the demarcation of the Santiago-Zamora sector in the Amazon region remained problematic due to a combination of alleged incomplete geographical information about this extremely remote area, and a growing reluctance among the military and other sectors of Ecuadorian society to accept the terms of the protocol.[29] Most clashes between the armies of both countries after the Rio Protocol would take place in that region, and it was the issue of "sovereign access to the Amazon" that would much later represent the last stone to be turned before a final peace could be reached.

The relations between Peru and Ecuador during the five decades between the celebration of the Rio Protocol and the Cenepa War would be dominated by the unfinished business at Ecuador's eastern border. Ecuador suspended the demarcation process in the disputed zone—particularly in the area of the Cordillera del Condor, where the arbitration suggested the boundary line should be—and declared the protocol to be infeasible given the incongruities between the formula established by the arbitration and the geographic realities on the ground. In 1960, President Velazco Ibarra of Ecuador declared the protocol null, establishing a position that would be reaffirmed by most of his successors until 1995. Peru's position was simply to maintain the validity and legality of the Rio Protocol, deny any real demarcation problems at the border, and accuse Ecuador of reneging on its obligations under the treaty. Both countries' positions crystallized over the years in seemingly opposite interpretations of the issue, the main point being the effectiveness of the protocol. The proximity of the army outposts of the opposing forces in the border area led to frequent skirmishes and occasional clashes, most of little consequence. In 1981, Peru's reaction to Ecuador's alleged construction of military outposts inside its territory led to the Paquisha Incident. In this instance, Ecuador requested the OAS to act as a mediator but was denied and forced to request the good offices of the "four friendly nations" who in fact constituted the guarantors of the Rio Protocol.[30] The reluctance of the OAS to become involved is characteristic of the preference of the continent's main powers for negotiating the issue within the framework of the protocol rather than within a collective security forum.

NOTES

1. For a brief and accurate account of the dispute's origins, see Ronald B. St. John, "The Boundary Between Ecuador and Peru," *Boundary and Territory Briefing* 1, 4 (1994).
2. David R. Mares counted eighty-three militarized disputes between Peru and Ecuador in the twentieth century alone to illustrate his argument for the existence of an enduring rivalry. Our argument considers the number of armed conflicts as a relevant variable in defining a rivalry but also introduces Vasquez's actor dimension and the concept of identity to explain the rivalry's logic, dynamics, and ending. D. Mares, *Violent Peace: Militarized Interstate Bargaining in Latin America* (New York: Columbia University Press, 2001).
3. Alexander B. Murphy, "The Sovereign State System as Political-Territorial Ideal: Historical and Contemporary Considerations," in T. J. Biersteker and C. Weber, eds., *State Sovereignty* (Cambridge: Cambridge University Press, 1996).
4. The manner in which Brazil won independence from Portugal can hardly be termed a revolution. Brazil's was also the only independence movement that conserved a monarchical regime in the midst of the republican effervescence of the time.
5. Murphy, "The Sovereign State System," p. 93.
6. Ibid., p. 93. "The spatial organization of society in west central Europe after the Peace of Westphalia fostered a world view in which discrete, quasi-independent territorial units were seen as the principal building blocks for social and political life. This political-geographic understanding is referred to as the *sovereign territorial ideal*."

7. Ibid., p. 91.
8. Kalevi J. Holsti, *The State, War and the State of War* (Cambridge: Cambridge University Press, 1996).
9. Robert H. Jackson, *Quasi-States: Sovereignty, International Relations and the Third World* (Cambridge: Cambridge University Press, 1990).
10. B. Anderson, *Imagined Communities: Reflections on the Origin and Spread of Nationalism* (London: Verso, 1991).
11. Sarah Radcliffe and Sallie Westwood, *Remaking the Nation: Place, Identity and Politics in Latin America* (London: Routledge, 1996).
12. Peter F. Klarén, *Peru: Society and Nationhood in the Andes* (Oxford: Oxford University Press, 2000).
13. Radcliffe and Westwood provided the characterization of Ecuador in *Remaking the Nation*, p. 61. Adrián Bonilla identified the "open wound" in *Fuerza, Conflicto y Negociacion*, p. 17.
14. St. John, "The Boundary Between Ecuador and Peru."
15. Ecuadorian historians would claim that the autonomy of Quito vis-à-vis Cuzco (Peru) established during the time of the Inca empire had precedence over the acts of the Spanish crown.
16. See map in the front matter of this book.
17. Klarén, *Peru: Society and Nationhood*.
18. Jacob Bercovitch, Paul F. Diehl, and Gary Goertz, "The Management and Termination of Protracted Interstate Conflicts: Conceptual and Empirical Considerations," *Millennium: Journal of International Studies* 26 (3), 1997.
19. Ibid., p. 760.
20. Ronald Bruce St. John, "Las Relaciones Ecuador y Perú: Una Perspectiva Histórica," in Adrián Bonilla, ed., *Ecuador-Perú: Horizontes de la Negociación y el Conflicto* (Quito: Flacso, 1999).
21. St. John, "The Boundary Between Ecuador and Peru."
22. Ibid., p. 9.
23. M. Biato, *O Processo de Paz Equador-Peru e a Solução Pacífica de Controvérsias* (Brazil: Instituto Rio Branco, 2001).
24. St. John, "'The Boundary Between Ecuador and Peru."
25. P. Calvert, *Boundary Disputes in Latin America*, quoted by K. J. Holsti, *The State, War and the State of War*, p. 153.
26. Klarén, *Peru: Society and Nationhood*.
27. President Carlos Arroyo del Rio was later overthrown in 1944 by the military. From 1931 to 1944 Ecuador had eighteen presidents, most of them unelected. Only four completed their terms. See Catherine M. Conaghan, "Floating Politicians and Institutional Stress: Presidentialism in Ecuador 1979–1988," in J. J. Linz and A. Valenzuela, eds., *The Failure of Presidential Democracy*, p. 256.
28. Jose Mighel Vásconeza Ribadeneira, "Del Protocolo de Rio de Janeiro a la Declaración Presidencial de Brasilia" (master's thesis, University of Brasilia, 2000), p. 170.

29. Ecuador would argue, after an aerial reconnaissance of the Santiago-Zamora region by the U.S. Air Force in 1949, that the extension of the Cenepa River exceeded what was represented in the maps used to draw the border established in the protocol. As a result, the protocol itself, from the Ecuadorian perspective, was not executable in that disputed area.

30. St. John, "The Boundary Between Ecuador and Peru," p. 100.

3

The Cenepa War

THE 1991 CRISIS

Ten years after the serious incident at Paquisha, a new crisis emerged in January 1991, in the Santiago-Zamora sector, over the location of new military outposts. From the broader perspective of the long-standing rivalry between Ecuador and Peru, the new episode appears to be another instance of heightened tension produced by troop movements in and around the disputed section of the border. Since the line of demarcation was the object of contending claims, accusations from both sides about occasional invasions by patrols or the construction of outposts within disputed territory were quite common. Indeed, the dynamics of the incident, and the fact that it took place in January, close to the anniversary of the signing of the Rio Protocol, suggested another of the routine militarized clashes characteristic of an enduring rivalry. However, some circumstantial factors indicated that its significance and outcome differed, in important ways, from those of previous incidents.

First, the Cold War was over and the "new world order" promised enhanced participation by the international community, through strengthened collective security organizations, in conflict mediation and resolution. The Gulf War produced a strong impression worldwide, especially upon third world countries facing potent conflict situations that seemed, at least temporarily—as the experience in Somalia would soon demonstrate—to fall within the security ambit of a new great power activism. In Latin America the initial perception of the new international context was that the autonomy of countries in the region to negotiate their interests was significantly reduced in a unipolar world.

The transformation of the international system caused by the end of the Cold War affected the perceptions and calculations of both Peruvian and Ecuadorian policymakers. Systemic changes, as Waltz has extensively argued, are rare. Moreover, external political shocks are usually a necessary condition for the termination of rivalries, and the events at the turn of the 1980s certainly qualify as shocks.[1] From a rational actor approach, systemic changes alter the payoff structures that constrain state strategies. A structuralist view would emphasize, as we have in many of our arguments, the structural effects on state identities and interests. In 1991, of course, nobody was certain of the direction in which world politics was tending: the reactions of Ecuador and Peru to the most recent crisis reflected that uncertainty. They combined stock responses to border clashes, developed over years of rivalry, with, we believe, genuine attempts at negotiation that had been absent at least since the years of the Washington Conference. The domestic scenario had changed significantly since the early 1980s, particularly, as we argue in Chapter 4, through the neoliberal shift in economic policies adopted in both countries and through relative consolidation of democratic transitions, despite recurrent institutional instability that expressed the fragility of the new democracies. These trends in domestic politics do not qualify as political shocks in the sense suggested by the literature on enduring rivalry. However, the dismantling of the old state apparata did produce considerable changes in both countries' polities and social fabric.

The crisis was caused by disagreements over the installation, by Peru, of the Pachacutec outpost, in the Cusumaza-Yaupi sector, in August 1991. This sector was included in the 1945 Braz Diaz de Aguiar Arbitral Award, but there were conflicting interpretations as to exactly where the demarcation line should pass. A tree had been used as a landmark for some fifteen years to indicate where the *hito 20* would hypothetically be, establishing, in practice, a line of status quo. The tree had disappeared, but the Ecuadorians argued that the landmark was still visible and sufficient to guide troop movements and the installation of outposts.[2] The Ecuadorians argued further that the installation of the Peruvian post was a violation of the line of status quo and responded by constructing lookout bases of their own in what Peru considered to be its territory. The pattern was similar to that of many other incidents but, at a certain point, the posts were at such a close distance that hostilities seemed inevitable. Through diplomatic negotiations, followed closely by the Brazilian government, which was called upon to help mediate the crisis, both parties reached the Acuerdo de Distension, also referred to as a "gentlemen's agreement," or *pacto de caballeros,* that mandated the withdrawal of troops, the reparation of the *hito 19,* a previously existing landmark that had deteriorated with time, and the removal of the Pachacutec outpost. Peru took the occasion to reiterate its adherence to the 1942 Rio Protocol, transmitting the text of the *pacto* to the Brazilian government with a request to forward it to the other guarantor countries.

Ecuador stood its ground, contesting any possible interpretation of the agreement as a recognition of the validity of the protocol, even though it accepted the good offices of the four guarantors, offered in a joint communiqué issued in Brasilia in September 1991. The potential implications of the agreement for the comprehensive border dispute contributed to its nonimplementation. Peru refused to remove its outpost unless Ecuador removed the Teniente Ortiz base, located, according to Ecuador, behind the line traced by the protocol.[3]

The significance of the 1991 crisis lies in the fact that, *with* the aid of the guarantors, especially Brazil and the United States, a likely military confrontation was avoided by diplomatic means. Two points are important to our argument. First, after a long period of paralysis and reaffirmation of the nullity of the protocol in 1983, Ecuador demonstrated a clear inclination toward a renewed effort at negotiating the conflict. Moreover, it did not reject the guarantor countries' good offices, although this gesture should not be interpreted as a modification of its previous position regarding the protocol itself. Ecuador's response to the events of 1995 went still further: it led to Ecuador's recognition of the four countries concerned as guarantors of the protocol. Second, on the Peruvian side, the guarantors' declaration calling on both sides to find peaceful means to reach a *final* and *lasting* solution to the "issue" could be interpreted as suggesting that the problem went beyond the straightforward implementation of the 1942 protocol and might require further negotiation. The pressures brought to bear on Peru by the United States in order to avoid a military response to the crisis also reflected a less tolerant international climate regarding armed confrontations in the hemisphere.

PREVIOUS ATTEMPTS AT NEGOTIATION

The events that followed the crisis of 1991 were the most significant attempts to reopen negotiations before the Brasilia process emerged after the Cenepa War. President Alberto Fujimori, since rising to power in 1990, had adopted a general foreign policy direction that favored the resolution of disputes with Peru's neighbors. In Ecuador, President Rodrigo Borja had also adopted a more assertive foreign policy that valued the country's participation in multilateral forums, such as the Andean Pact. Indeed, the Cartagena Declaration on Security and Cooperation had been ratified by both countries in 1990 as a first effort to introduce political issues onto the agenda of the integration process. The declaration itself enjoyed little support in either country because the overarching question of the territorial dispute continued to frame relations. In any case, the avoidance of an armed confrontation, thanks to the gentlemen's agreement along with the international and domestic conditions mentioned earlier, seems to have contributed to the beginning of an exchange of ideas and proposals among the presidents that today may be interpreted as the initial signs of a change in attitude that would later contribute to the final peace agreement.

With the border incident still fresh in his mind, the Ecuadorian president presented his proposal for an arbitration, by Pope John Paul II, of all outstanding issues at the United Nations General Assembly. Borja's initiative produced some sympathy in the international community, and was inspired by the pope's successful mediation of the Beagle Channel crisis in 1979, when Argentina and Chile nearly went to war. Even though the proposal did not prosper, it produced a response from President Fujimori in October, who offered to present a counterproposal.

The talks led to the Peruvian president's visit to Quito, in January 1992, the first in the history of the countries' relationship. Fujimori presented a comprehensive proposal that included the demarcation of the border according to the Rio Protocol but with the technical assistance of the Vatican to mediate controversies, the signing of a treaty on navigation rights that included the creation of trading posts in the Amazon under Ecuadorian control, and an initiative to promote the economic integration of both countries.[4] It was still distant from the Ecuadorian plan presented at the UN, but the counterproposal was a departure from Peru's previously rigid support for the provisions contained in the protocol.

The new attitude was, seemingly, to recognize that a problem existed and that concessions had to be made if the issue was to be settled. While the negotiations met resistance and suspicions among some sectors of the public—particularly the foreign offices and the military, which held traditional views of the territorial problem—the presidents seem to have developed a degree of mutual trust that permitted guarded optimism.

The process ultimately failed due to developments in domestic politics in Peru and Ecuador (see Chapter 4). It was, however, an experience that signaled the possibility of a change in the actor dimension that fueled the enduring rivalry: the prospect of a gradual shift in perceptions of the other as the untrustworthy and perpetually threatening enemy. Some Ecuadorian critics have suggested that Fujimori was merely buying time, while preparing for the attack that took place in 1995.[5] The same accusation could be made against Ecuador, as it has been by authors such as David Mares, who believes Ecuador had the incentives and the design to use force as a negotiating tool, particularly after its defeat in 1981. The evidence for such claims is difficult to obtain and assess. While we have chosen not to debate the issue of who was responsible for the outbreak of the Cenepa War, we did not, in our research and interviews, uncover any evidence that would suggest that the negotiations in 1991–1992 were mere diversions. Their failure was, in our view, the result of political circumstances, and of the logic of enduring rivalry itself, which crushes every political effort beneath the inescapable and overwhelming weight of history. As the conditions on the ground remained essentially unaltered due to the ineffectiveness of the gentlemen's agreement, and as the expectations created by the bilateral negotiations remained unfulfilled, there was ample opportunity for the outbreak of new confrontations.

THE OUTBREAK OF WAR

The Cenepa War began on January 26, 1995, when Ecuadorian troops set in motion an operation to dislodge the Peruvian army from the camp of Base Norte, located on the eastern side of the Condor Ridge, at the source of the Cenepa River, in the Santiago-Zamora sector of the 78-kilometer disputed border. Combat lasted for over an hour. A Peruvian officer lost his life, and the Ecuadorians took some prisoners. Colonel Luis Aguas Navarez, of the Ecuadorian special forces, headed the patrol. He had been in the Upper Cenepa valley since December 1994, conducting field reconnaissance for a month.

The possibility of war was, at that time, present in his mind and the minds of his commanders because, as he stated, the "Peruvians were consolidating their positions within territory that had been Ecuador's for many years."[6] Base Norte was a rough opening in the Amazon jungle whither a detachment of around twenty Peruvian soldiers had recently been transported. The Ecuadorians discovered the camp a few days before, after noticing transport helicopters heading toward the northern side of the valley. There were Peruvian outposts located south of the three Ecuadorian camps of Tiwintza, Base Sur, and Coangos. When soldiers at these camps spotted Peruvian troops up the river, their movement was interpreted as part of an offensive strategy to remove the three Ecuadorian outposts (which had been constructed after the 1991 crisis). During the weeks that preceded the conflict, the troops from both armies continued to meet at *Cueva de los Tayos* as part of the confidence and security procedures established in earlier years to avoid unwanted patrol skirmishes. It was during one of those meetings, at the end of December 1994, that, according to Ecuadorian accounts, a Peruvian colonel issued an "ultimatum" threatening to use force unless the three outposts were abandoned. The Ecuadorian officers interviewed for this research, including the commanding officer in the field, Colonel Luis Hernandez, concurred in identifying the ultimatum as an indication that the Peruvians were preparing for war, triggering Ecuadorian preparation of military operations aimed at resisting a possible attack.

The rationale behind the ultimatum was not totally clear, but our interviewees considered it a political maneuver by the Peruvian president, who was then running for his second term, to gain domestic support in regions where he was uncertain about his electoral performance. Even ignoring the conspiratorial logic surrounding this argument, it is difficult to understand why Fujimori would need to start a war to win an election that was almost certainly to go his way, both because he was popular at the time and because he controlled the machinery of government and the electoral justice system in a manner that would guarantee his victory. Moreover, the absence of logistical support, adequate preparations, and experienced troops was a poor indicator of an offensive strategy unless the Peruvians grossly underestimated the Ecuadorian army. It is true that the military had gained considerable political influence under Fujimori's authoritarian rule after the 1992 *autogolpe*, but much of their resources was geared to fighting the Sendero Luminoso guerrilla movement (although, by 1995, most of its leadership had been captured or killed). In any case, there seems to have been a perception in the Ecuadorian government and particularly in the military that there was no intention on Peru's part to recover the negotiating effort of the early 1990s, and that tensions along the border were increasing due to the unresolved business of the 1991 crisis and to the overall instability caused by the open border.

There is evidence that the Ecuadorian military decided to strengthen its defensive capabilities in the area after their embarrassing performance in 1981 and their evident weakness during the 1991 incident. Decisions to construct the outposts were taken in the 1980s as part of that strategy. The problem in 1991 was a precursor of future developments produced by the policy of occupation of disputed areas.[7] Does this mean that the Ecuadorian army had been planning the war all along? We do not have an answer to that question except that it is unlikely. Under conditions of enduring rivalry that involve territorial disputes, the use of force is *always* a possibility because it becomes a recurrent means of dealing with an issue that can neither be adequately managed nor resolved through negotiations.

Another important question is, Why did another border clash escalate into a minor war? The most likely reason is the readiness of the Ecuadorian army, a factor that had previously been absent. It had become more professional, had acquired antiaircraft defenses from Nicaragua and jet fighters from Israel, and had trained its special forces for jungle fighting in places such as El Salvador. In the early days of the war, the Ecuadorians stood their ground and inflicted considerable losses upon the Peruvian army. They also brought down seven enemy aircraft, including a Soviet-made jet fighter, causing significant embarrassment to President Fujimori who, under criticism from the press and the opposition, and to show support to the troops, was bold enough to visit combat areas deep in the region of the Upper Cenepa.

The escalation of hostilities can also be explained by the opportunity the conflict presented Ecuador to measure up its forces in more favorable settings and conditions, and establish a more balanced situation on the ground. The opportunity also to redress a history of humiliating defeats must not be underestimated. The military had considerable autonomy in the decisionmaking process to determine a response to the perceived new threat from Peru. The operation to dislodge the Peruvian detachment from Base Norte had already been authorized before the president and the security council were informed that it was actually under way on the afternoon of January 26, 1995. According to Adrián Bonilla, the decision to use force resulted from "previous events that escaped the control of civilian authorities."[8]

Furthermore, Borja's successor, President Duran Ballen (1992–1996), had a notoriously erratic and reactive foreign policy. On the issue of the border conflict, Ballen abandoned his predecessor's policies to construct a negotiation-friendly environment and simply reaffirmed traditional objections to the Rio Protocol and claims to redress the injustices of the past. President Ballen also suffered from a lack of domestic support caused, among other things, by the negative effects of his orthodox economic policies.

It is striking that when the first hostilities erupted, very little effort was made through diplomatic channels to avoid the escalation of the conflict. Former defense minister General José Gallardo argued that the failure of General Nicolas de Bari Hermosa—his Peruvian counterpart—to respond to several attempts to establish communications in order to discuss the situation on the ground represented a strong indication of the Peruvian government's negative attitude toward a peaceful resolution of the new crisis. Hermosa's silence was mentioned by several other Ecuadorian army officers as a determinant in the decisionmaking process that led to offensive action against the Peruvian "invasion."[9] Gallardo made no reference, however, to any other channels being activated to defuse the situation. It is likely that there were none, since the civilian authorities did not participate directly in the decisions and could not possibly have interfered to stop what was now a confrontation already in process. On the other hand, it was not in Ecuador's interest to escalate the war *outside* the Upper Cenepa region, that is, along the rest of the Peru-Ecuador border, particularly in the lowlands closer to the Pacific. That was where the Peruvian army had obtained its victory in 1941 with extreme ease, and where it still enjoyed overwhelming superiority. Fear of a general escalation certainly contributed to limiting the scale of violence and to attempts to end the war quickly. The guarantor countries issued declarations to the parties urging them to refrain from the use of force as early as January 27. Ecuador had also requested Brazil's mediation to help restore peace. Talks took place in Brasilia during February, the month in which most of the fighting took place. On February 17, the parties and the guarantor countries signed the Peace Declaration of Itamaraty, which established an immediate cease-fire, and agreed on the initiation of talks. Fighting continued, however, until the end of the month when, threatening to withdraw their support from the conflict resolution effort, the guarantors forced the parties to sign the Declaration of Montevideo, on February 28, 1995, which consolidated the cease-fire and authorized the deployment of military observers to the region.

There are no reliable sources for the number of casualties in the Cenepa War. Bonilla estimates deaths at 1,500, based on confidential reports from Ecuadorian officers. Generals Gallardo and Paco Moncayo, respectively defense minister and army commander at the time; Colonel Luis Hernandez, commander of one of the main units involved in the fighting; and Lieutenant-Colonel Luis Aguas, who also participated directly in operations, considered that number extremely high and agreed roughly on no more than 500 casualties, most of them on the Peruvian side. We had no access to Peruvian estimates of casualties. The conflict does qualify as a war, however, given the level of mobilization of the armed forces, the risk of escalation, and the relevance of the issue for the national security of both countries in a long history of rivalry. The new international and regional context in which the war occurred contributed to a more decisive involvement on the part of the guarantor countries, which dedicated a level of attention and political investment that had been absent during the previous five decades. It also established a new context in which negotiations would now take place and would lead to the apparent resolution of the territorial dispute at the heart of the rivalry, with the signature of the Brasilia Accords. It is to the actual process that began after the war of 1995 that we now turn.

NOTES

1. Jacob Bercovitch, Paul Diehl, and Gary Goertz, "The Management and Termination of Protracted Interstate Conflicts: Conceptual and Empirical Considerations," *Millennium: Journal of International Studies* 26, 3 (1997).

2. Diego Cordovez, *Nuestra Propuesta Inconclusa: Ecuador-Perú: Del Inmovilismo al Acuerdo de Brasilia* (Quito: Corporación Editora Nacional, 2000).

3. Ibid., pp. 28–37. See also Jose Mighel Vásconeza Ribadeneira, "Del

Protocolo de Rio de Janeiro a la Declaración Presidencial de Brasilia" (master's thesis, University of Brasilia, 2000).

4. Ministerio de Relaciones Exteriores, "Contrapropuesia Peruana 1992," Quito, 1992, quoted in Cordovez, *Nuestra Propuesta,* p. 46.

5. Confidential interview with Ecuadorian army officer, Quito, April 2001.

6. Interview with Colonel Luis Aguas, Quito, April 2001.

7. Adrián Bonilla, "Proceso Politico e Intereses Nacionales en el Conflicto Peru-Ecuador," *Nueva Sociedad* 143 (1996): 30–40.

8. Bonilla, "Proceso Politico," p. 39.

9. Interview with General Jose Gallardo, Quito, April 2001.

4

The Mediation Process

Between 1995 and 1998, a concerted effort took place involving the countries in conflict and the four mediating countries, Brazil, Chile, Argentina, and the United States, that led to the final settlement of a dispute that dated back to colonial times. Whereas since the 1940s the temporary demilitarization of the area had been the most significant achievement of the negotiations, during this period the concrete issues that divided Peru and Ecuador were tackled. Despite the existence of provisions in the inter-American system for the settlement of disputes, the mediation process was based on the provisions established by the 1942 Rio de Janeiro Protocol. This framework determined that the four countries mentioned, under Brazilian coordination, were to mediate the dispute.

The basic divergence between the parties was that the Peruvians favored a complete demarcation of the border, as established in the 1942 Rio Protocol, while Ecuador stated that the protocol was partially inexecutable and that Ecuador must have free and sovereign access to the Marañon and Amazon Rivers. Peru maintained that the protocol, its complementary provisions, and the award of the Brazilian arbiter Captain Braz Diaz de Aguiar permitted a final border demarcation.

In fact, one of the most difficult divergences to be dealt with at the beginning of the negotiations and throughout the process was the difference in positions regarding the 1942 protocol. Throughout the process, the guarantors were concerned with coordinating the military with the political dimensions of reconstructing bilateral relations. They therefore focused on the role of the Military Observation Mission Ecuador Peru (MOMEP), on the changing atti-

49

tudes of the military establishments in both countries, and on the danger of an arms race. Regarding this last concern, they urged all other countries not to sell arms to Peru or Ecuador until a final agreement was reached.[1] Still, the danger of further violence was always present, particularly when the process stalled or when domestic opposition to the peace agreement caused internal instability in either country.

In this chapter we start by recapitulating the events and procedures that distinguished the international negotiations. The main features of the observation mission are then described. An analysis follows of the domestic and regional security environments that set the limits and possibilities of the mediation process. Finally, we investigate the main concepts and methods that sustained this multilateral effort.

REVIEW OF THE 1995–1998 MEDIATION PROCESS

On January 23, 1995, the Ecuadorian president summoned the ambassadors of the guarantor countries, requesting their attention in view of the seriousness of the Cenepa situation. A few days later the representatives of Chile, Argentina, the United States, and Brazil met in Brasilia, issuing declarations that reaffirmed their responsibilities regarding the conflict and their determination to find a definite solution to the dispute.[2] While Melvyn deVitsky, representing the United States, and the vice foreign ministers of Chile, Argentina, and Brazil met in Brasilia, the OAS summoned a consultative meeting of foreign ministers to consider the gravity of the situation.[3] Although the guarantors rapidly became involved in containing the crisis, it should be mentioned that Ecuador did send a communiqué to the president of the Security Council of the United Nations and requested an extraordinary meeting of the Permanent Council of the OAS. Cesar Gaviria, the OAS secretary-general, traveled both to Quito and to Lima offering his good offices.[4]

The severity of the situation at this moment should be stressed. As the diplomats involved in this crisis management exercise remarked in several interviews, the possibility of escalation had to be considered. Initial negotiations for a cease-fire were not easy, the Peruvians aiming to return to the status quo ante and the Ecuadorians trying to secure their strategic gains. A cease-fire accord was reached only ten days after the issuing of the Itamaraty Declaration, on February 17, 1995.

Although Ecuador did accomplish a small victory in the Cenepa region, the balance of power clearly favored Peru. The Peruvian weapon procurements that followed the conflict and the economic cost of the war effort for Ecuador made this reality clear. In this context, the only mediation instrument available could not be dismissed by the Ecuadorian government. In fact, when the parties met in Rio de Janeiro on January 31, 1995, to negotiate a cease-fire, the guarantors, and consequently the protocol, were being re-established as the only multilateral peacemaking mechanism for this case. This was an opportunity for Ecuador to reopen a debate in which it was the revisionist state. Satisfaction can be detected in the words of Marcelo Fernández de Córdoba, Ecuadorian representative to the Brasilia negotiations: "It was the beginning of a new era in which Ecuador could and should assert its rights gained through centuries of history and find a definite solution to its territorial problem."[5]

Nevertheless, the negotiations became possible within this framework only because the Ecuadorian government decided in February 1995 that the protocol was in force, although it was not executable in the basins of the Cenepa, Santiago, and Zamora Rivers for historical reasons and due to references to nonexistent geographic features.[6] Henceforth Brazil, Chile, the United States, and Argentina would no longer be referred to solely as "friendly countries." The importance of this decision should not be overlooked since, as we have seen, the status of the protocol was a central idea in Ecuador's foreign policy formulations. The positions Ecuador adopted in multilateral forums often reflected this concern. For instance, in 1968 Ecuador proposed an amendment to the Vienna Conference on Treaty Rights, which became Article 42 of the Vienna Convention on Treaty Rights, referring to the nullity of treaties obtained by the threat or the use of force.[7] Ecuador also refrained from signing the 1948 Pact of Bogotá, which called for mandatory conflict management.

From the other side of the negotiating table, the Peruvian government recognized that the protocol did not encompass all pending issues and that simply to conclude the demarcation of the border was not an option. The incorporation of the term *subsistent impasses* in the Itamaraty Declaration opened the door to subsequent review of the protocol.[8] Nevertheless, when discussions on procedures were under way in 1996, Ecuador and Peru disagreed on the role to be

played by the guarantors, the Ecuadorian negotiators having supported the possibility of arbitration by other actors, while the Peruvian
representatives favored a definitive solution based on the protocol.[9]
The issue of arbitration divided the parties since the Peruvian position was that the Diaz de Aguiar Award had already settled the
demarcation of the border and that the protocol was a perfect juridical instrument; hence no further arbitration was necessary. At the
Lima meeting in January 1996, Galo Leoro, the Ecuadorian foreign
minister, referred to the possible use of an arbiter or facilitator;[10] at
the Buenos Aires meeting in June 1996, Ecuadorian negotiators criticized the definition of the Rio Protocol as the sole framework for
discussions since this greatly limited their possibilities for
maneuver.[11]

Meanwhile, the meeting held in Brasilia in February 1995, following earlier negotiations in Rio de Janeiro between the deputy foreign ministers of both Ecuador and Peru, established that the peace
process would develop in three stages: the stabilization of the military situation, the procedural definition of the outstanding points of
disagreement, and finally the substantive negotiations on issues
defined at the previous stage. On February 17, 1995, the parties
signed the Itamaraty Peace Declaration,[12] which sets out a framework for negotiations. The declaration establishes a cease-fire from
February 14 onward, the organization and deployment of a military
observation mission, the separation of forces, the creation of a demilitarized zone, the gradual and reciprocal demobilization of military
units, and the initiation of talks.

Yet the second half of 1995 was marked by uncertainty due to
the governmental transition in Ecuador and the Peruvian preference
for waiting to negotiate with the new government. The generation of
tension within the Ecuadorian military establishment at this point
was a real possibility. General Moncayo defended the recourse to
arbitration, signaling that sectors within the army were clearly
unhappy with the ongoing process.[13]

At the beginning of 1996, the second stage of the mediation
process started. The first meeting involving the foreign ministers of
Peru and Ecuador and diplomats from the guarantor countries took
place in Lima on January 17 and 18. Several procedural arrangements were agreed upon: Brasilia was designated the venue for negotiations, each delegation was to be composed of five delegates, there
would be no fixed timetable, the negotiations would be secret, and

the observation mission would stay in place. During this meeting the Peruvian foreign minister, Francisco Tudela, stressed the difference between political and juridical issues: this argument remained current throughout the negotiation process.[14] Although Ecuador had at this point accepted the protocol framework as a basis for negotiations, its status was not yet clearly defined, the Peruvian foreign minister having stressed that no further arbitration was necessary and the Ecuadorian foreign minister having favored mandatory proposals by the guarantors. Finally, Tudela agreed not to veto any apparently political "impasses" presented by the Ecuadorian side, and Ecuador agreed that the recommendations made by the mediators were not mandatory.

The Lima meeting and the February meeting, which was hosted in Quito, allowed for the definition of important procedures. In addition to the procedural arrangements for the negotiations, a bilateral commission to oversee arms purchases and a joint military working group to enhance security and stability were created,[15] and the parties clearly defined their disagreements. The Quito Accord summarizes these procedural agreements. The lists of impasses were presented by both parties on March 6 in Brasilia.

The parties only reached a final agreement on the procedures for negotiations after a meeting in Buenos Aires in June and one in Santiago in October. Substantive negotiations were to begin before the end of 1996 and were to be continuous until a final resolution. The principle of single undertaking was to be adopted, the parties would outline points of agreement and disagreement, and the guarantors would require compliance with agreements and suggest solutions when necessary. Issues would be discussed sequentially starting with those that presented fewer difficulties.[16] The parties were to negotiate directly and the guarantors were to present recommendations; issues could be referred to the guarantors, and the acceptance of proposals made by the guarantors was entirely in the hands of Peru and Ecuador.

It is interesting to note that in addition to the 1942 Rio Protocol, this phase of the negotiations added four further documents to the basic framework of the negotiations.[17] The Santiago Accord established that the guarantors would assume the responsibility of "proposing the procedures most adequate for the definite resolution of points of disagreement that the parts have not been successful in dealing with directly."[18] In contrast, Article 7 of the 1942 protocol states that "any doubt or disagreement that arises regarding the execution of this Protocol will be resolved by the parties with the support of the representatives of the United States, Argentina, Brazil, and Chile."[19] Thus, although the guarantors did not assume the role of arbiters, a position the Ecuadorians had argued for, they did assume a more active role than originally planned.

The list of impasses delivered at the February meeting in Quito to Ambassador Ivan Canabrava, the Brazilian representative in these talks, established the subject of future negotiations. It was agreed that no further issues could be added to this list. Ecuador's list presented the following problems: the 1942 protocol was partially not executable due to the absence of a watershed *(divortium acquarium)* between the Zamora and Santiago Rivers; free access and sovereignty over the Marañon River; the demarcation of the Cusumaza Bumbuiza-Yaupi sector and Lagartocasha-Guepi sector; problems where rivers were intersected by the survey lines; problems regarding the Napo River; and the blockage of the Zarumilla Canal.[20] Peru, by contrast, stressed the necessity of the demarcation of the border, as established by Article 8 of the Rio Protocol.

In April 1997, after a period of confusion marked by the occupation of the Japanese embassy in Lima and the fall of Abdala Bucaram,[21] substantive talks began in Brasilia. During the following six months the wider objectives of the disputants were enlarged upon and discussed. Six rounds of negotiations took place between April and November of that same year. During this period the tendency observed earlier, wherein Peruvian arguments were expressed in technical and juridical terms and Ecuadorian arguments were phrased in political terms, persisted.[22] These negotiations were disturbed by the resignation of Peru's foreign minister, Francisco Tudela, and the president of that country's delegation, Alfonso Arias Schriber, and by tensions on the frontier.

In November 1997, when the sixth round of talks in this phase took place, the guarantors decided to take a more active role, suggesting the division of the talks into four major camps, which would correspond to the commissions created during the following year. At this point, the guarantors, drawing on the provisions of the Santiago Accord, made proposals that would head the negotiations in a new direction, enabling the common interests of the disputants and the potential advantages of cooperation to emerge. The two delegations received a document that restated the responsibilities of the guarantors and contained substantive proposals regarding the use of the Amazon Basin, border integration and development, confidence building, and border demarcation.[23]

In January 1998, the Rio de Janeiro schedule was approved, according to which the four commissions were each to work on relevant issues. In the document outlining the schedule, in contrast to the document presented in November, no mention was made of the status of areas already demarcated or of access to the Amazon Basin. The negotiations leading to the definition of the Rio de Janeiro schedule were not easy, Fernández de Córdoba having left the negotiation process and Eduarco Ferrero Costa having made allusion to the role of the mediators as guarantors of a juridical instrument, not of an international peace process.[24]

Four commissions, one working group, and a mechanism of evaluation by the foreign ministries of Peru and Ecuador were created and procedures were established. The structuring of the commissions was based on the idea that the mutual benefits of cooperation and integrated development should be stressed. The navigation and commerce commission was to meet in Buenos Aires (Commission I), the border economic integration commission in Washington (Commission II), the land border demarcation commission in Brasilia (Commission III), and the confidence- and security-building measures commission in Santiago (Commission IV).

Commission II worked on the elaboration of a project for economic development in the area and the administration of the border basin. Four plenary meetings took place in Washington, D.C., where international financial institutions were more readily available, and thirteen binational work groups also met, exchanging views between Quito and Lima. The development of the border area in general, the intensification of commerce between the two countries, and the creation of a community of interests were the purposes behind the propositions discussed. In contrast with the other three commissions, which were to deal with the contentions between the two countries, this group was given a mandate to be "creative, optimistic and ambitious."[25]

The confidence-building and security commission aimed at the generation of a binational commission on that subject, as outlined in the Brasilia Declaration. The binational commission was made permanent in May 1998, during a meeting in Santiago. Previous conversations between the high commands of both countries and existing bilateral mechanisms for confidence building between the two armies facilitated this decision and its implementation. In fact, this had been a theme of the two countries' relations since 1967, the documents "procedures of engagement and information" and "manual for norms of behavior" having been produced in 1967 and 1984. Twenty-two meetings took place between the two armies from 1967 to 1995.[26] After the 1981 Paquisha Incident, there was additional concern in generating rules for the troops allocated near the border, although these measures did not prevent the 1991 incident near Teniente Ortiz. It should be noted that the contact and flow of information made available in this case, fundamentally concerning procedures, pertain to first-generation confidence-building measures.[27] Obviously these were ineffectual in preventing the violent clashes of 1995.

Apart from the general aim of generating confidence and avoiding misperceptions that may lead to hostilities, the commission was to assist in the development of activities involving other sectors in both societies that would enhance communication and confidence.[28] There was some disagreement here between the parties, Ecuador having defended a broader definition than Peru of security and a wider range of activities for the commission. In the end, the seven articles of the accord dealt with cooperation in areas related to the military dimension but focused on a more traditional definition of security.

The navigation and commerce commission, which met between February and September 1998, was to generate a commerce and navigation treaty, allowing for free access to the Amazon Basin, port facilities, and customs benefits; deal with the difficulties generated by the fact that some rivers cut across international borders; and generate projects facilitating terrestrial communication and navigation in the sectors where rivers were diverted along the Napo River. The establishment of a navigation treaty is foreseen in the 1942 protocol (Article 6).[29] This was an extremely relevant issue for Ecuador since it potentially allowed for free access to the Marañon-Amazon basin and could thus permit the country to enjoy its full status as an "Amazonian country," a concept that is central to the definition of Ecuadorian national identity. Two areas were of particular concern to Ecuador: the survey lines of Yaupi-Bobonaza, Pastaza-Tigre and Tigre-Cononac, and the Napo River (Yasuni-Aguarico sector). Free access to certain rivers, as set out in the 1942 protocol, was not a possibility since the international border crossed the river several times. As a result of the work of this commission, the principle that the border could not be changed was respected. On the other hand, the principle of free navigation was upheld.

The establishment of two Ecuadorian facilities for trade and navigation in Peru, linked by road to that country, was to overcome the isolation caused by the fact that the Amazonian rivers were not suited for navigation on the Ecuadorian side of the border. Ecuador tried to bring into the debate the concept of *functional sovereignty*, whereby some European states shared the use of natural resources. As Marcel Biato reports, the Peruvian position was that these centers would represent a transgression of Peruvian sovereignty. The definition of jurisdiction over these enclaves was thus a crucial question, and the creation of a free port was unacceptable to Peru.[30]

The commission on border demarcation determined that a group of specialists, including Peruvian and Ecuadorian nationals, would present a report on the territorial issue. The specialists dealt with three different sectors of the border: the Lagartococha sector, the Cusumaza-Bumbuiza–Santiago-Yaupi confluence, and the Cunhuime Sur–20 de Noviembre sector. Ecuador had rejected the Dias de Aguiar arbitration award, which the experts confirmed regarding the Lagartococha sector and the Cunhuime Sur–20 de Noviembre sector. The view of the specialists regarding the demarcation of the Cusumaza-Bumbuiza–Santiago-Yaupi confluence, which generated disagreement in the context of the mixed commission on border demarcation, was accepted by both parties. A distinction was established between cartographic and historical criteria, allowing for the Ecuadorian post of Teniente Ortiz, established since the 1930s, to remain within that country's borders. In the case of the Cunhuime Sur–20 de Noviembre sector, the demarcation was more sensitive as Ecuador maintained that the fact that there is no watershed between the Zamora and Santiago Rivers in this area meant that the Rio Protocol could not be executed. Ecuador's position was that the true extent of the Cenepa River became clear only after the 1947 cartographic survey made by the U.S. Air Force at the request of both parties. Peru countered that the extent of the river was irrelevant as far as the existence of a watershed between the Santiago and the Zamora Rivers was concerned.[31] Thus the demarcation of the Alto Cenepa area was not consensual, Ecuadorian representatives having decided not to accept the position presented in June by the remaining specialists. In effect, the commission validated the Peruvian claim, generating fierce opposition in Ecuador. Ecuador at this point faced presidential elections. The disputants therefore left the 78-kilometer border demarcation problem to be tackled at the end of the process.

A working group on the Zarumilla Canal was also created, meeting between March and April 1998. Ever since the Zarumilla Canal was established as the border between Peru and Ecuador, variations in its route had generated demarcation problems. The Diaz de Aguiar Award established the route at a location different from that found at the time of negotiations. Furthermore, the Peruvian government did not undertake the work necessary to give the Ecuadorian population, dependent on the canal for irrigation, access to a supply of water, as envisaged in the Aguiar award. In this case Ecuador demanded respect for the findings of the award. A permanent commission was created to guarantee the best utilization of the canal waters.[32]

The discussions on border integration and confidence building did not generate greater tension. But the negotiations regarding commerce and navigation and the demarcation of the border tackled the sensitive issues—the access to the Amazon Basin and the criteria for a final border demarcation—on which the parties had stood opposed for many years. It would not be possible to reach a conclusion on these two issues separately. The Peruvian government would only accept compromises regarding access to the Amazon Basin if a final chapter could be written on the demarcation of the bilateral border. In this context, the public presentation of the accords reached by the border integration commission in both Quito and Lima aimed at highlighting the positive aspects of the redefinition of bilateral relations.[33]

The negotiations that followed in June and July were affected by the political vacuum in Ecuador, the change of government, and the standoff regarding the specialists' report on border demarcation. The infiltration of Ecuadorian troops south of the demilitarized zone and the mobilization of troops on the border area threatened the whole negotiation process. A visit to Quito planned by President Fujimori on the occasion of Jamil Mahuad's inauguration was canceled.[34] Finally, an agreement on the separation of forces was reached, and both the Peruvian foreign minister, Eduardo Ferrero Costa, and the commander in chief of the armed forces, Nicolás Hermoza de Bari, who had defended the use of force to dislodge Ecuadorian troops, left the government.[35]

After the 1998 crisis, when troops were mobilized, presidential diplomacy played a crucial role in the negotiations. After taking office, the new Ecuadorian president, Jamil Mahuad, accepted the outcome of the technical reviews and established a working relationship with his counterpart, Alberto Fujimori.

The new Ecuadorian president, who had been inaugurated on August 10, 1998, met with Alberto Fujimori seven times between August and September at several locations, consolidating a commitment to a definite solution, although they did not come to an agreement on the outstanding territorial issue.[36] On September 14, an agreement on the content of the Treaty on Commerce and Navigation was announced.[37] The following month, both presidents asked the guarantor states to assume binding arbitration on the issues on which they could not reach agreement. After the congresses of both Peru and Ecuador had approved resolutions expressing their agreement with the mandatory character of the proposal on October 16,[38] the guarantors concurred. On October 23, Presidents Fernando Henrique Cardoso, Bill Clinton, Carlos Menem, and Eduardo Frei submitted a letter to the presidents of Ecuador and Peru containing a proposal, which was accepted. The principle of *single undertaking,* which had structured the negotiations, having been met, the Act of Brasilia was then signed by the parties. Six bilateral accords were signed on October 26, 1998: the Treaty on Commerce and Navigation, the Border Integration Accord, the Bilateral Commission on Confidence Building Measures, the Accord on the Zarumilla Canal, and the Border Demarcation Agreement. Apart from the global accord on peace, the agreements reached were to be subject to vote by the legislatures of both countries.

By the terms of these final agreements, the border between the two countries was to be demarcated, but a flexible interpretation of the concept of sovereignty allowed for an accommodation of both parties' demands.[39] Although the demarcation process was to respect the principles of the 1942 protocol, the Condor Ridge having been defined as the frontier line, the access and rights of sovereignty in the area were redefined in a more complex manner. Ecuador was to have access to Peru's Amazon tributaries, and two facilities for trade and navigation were to be made available, thereby implementing Article 6 of the Rio Protocol. These centers were bestowed upon Ecuador for a period of fifty years; they were subject to Peruvian legislation and were to be administered by private firms. Ecuador was to designate an official responsible for commerce and navigation, whose status was to be ruled by the Vienna Convention on Consulate Officials. Ecuadorians would thus reach the Atlantic Ocean from domestic waters, and Ecuador would partially fulfill its identity as an Amazon country, while Peru would preserve its sovereign rights in these areas.[40]

The Treaty on Commerce and Navigation, furthermore, established that Ecuador and Peru would mutually bestow upon each other the status of most-favored nation, specifically regarding pluvial navigation, land transit, and commercial facilities. Ecuadorian vessels were to receive the same treatment as Peruvian vessels. This allowed Ecuador to take part in the potential economic integration of the region.

Two demilitarized ecological parks were to be created, one in each of the contending countries, in the Upper Cenepa region. The Peruvian government was committed by the treaty to allow free navigation and circulation of Ecuadorian nationals on the Napo River. Peru was also obliged to guarantee that river waters would flow through the Zarumilla Canal, the distribution of the water flux having been established as 55 percent for Peru and 45 percent for Ecuador, thus ensuring a supply of water for the Ecuadorian population living on the riverside.

Ecuador also acquired perpetual access to Tiwintza, the site of a battle in February 1995. At this site, where Ecuadorian soldiers are buried, it would be possible to honor the heroes of that battle. Nevertheless, rights of sovereignty, such as stationing police and troops or conducting commercial activities, could not be exercised in this area. Ecuador was granted the rights established by Peruvian private law in this area, which covers one square kilometer. Peru was obliged to construct and maintain a road between Tiwintza and Ecuadorian territory.

Finally, an economic development and integration program coordinated with the Inter-American Development Bank was created. Projects with a projected value of U.S.$3 billion were to be executed over the following ten years. The border integration accord foresaw a plan for the development of the area, the organization of a fund for that purpose, and projects in several areas such as transportation, electricity, tourism, fisheries, and education. A neighborhood commission was created to prepare programs and projects reflecting the common interests of the two countries. The promotion of private investment in the border area and the intensification of commerce between the two countries were to be promoted by working groups; by the binational fund for peace and development; by a project for the liberalization of commerce, including measures regarding technical and bureaucratic procedures; by programs for the development of infrastructure in the border area; and by sector-specific agreements. The fund, which was to be directed by an executive organ composed of eight members, half from each country, was to issue a Peace and Development Certificate for every U.S.$5 million received.[41]

In January 1999, the two countries restarted the demarcation of the border. In May that year the demarcation was finalized, the Ecuadorian and Peruvian presidents signed an integration accord, and Tiwintza was handed over to Ecuador.

THE MILITARY OBSERVER MISSION
ECUADOR PERU

The Military Observer Mission Ecuador Peru (MOMEP) was the first multilateral peace operation established in South America, apart from a military observer mission sent to Leticia in 1934.[42] The mandate of the mission was to observe and verify compliance with the terms of the Brasilia Accords.[43] The initial objective was to guarantee the cessation of hostilities, but the main purpose of the operation was to insulate the diplomatic negotiations that took place throughout the period from the confrontation on the ground. The mission also had the aim of generating confidence between the parties. A committee consisting of representatives of the four guarantors exercised political control of the mission; it was coordinated by a Brazilian general, who exercised operational control, throughout the process.[44] It was installed both at the permanent operation center of Coangos, in Ecuador, and at Puesto de Vigilancia 1 (PV1), in Peru.

As mentioned earlier, the cease-fire negotiations were difficult, hostilities having continued after the issuing of the Itamaraty Declaration in February. The mission was organized only after a further commitment on the cessation of violence was made, in Montevideo ten days later, at the inauguration of President Julio María Sanguinetti.[45]

In March 1995, the separation of forces began, and the procedures to be observed by the mission were defined. A document was signed on March 10 in Brasilia establishing support for the mission by both the Peruvian and Ecuadorian armies. Thus, the first observers arrived on the ground on March 12 under the coordination of General Candido Vargas de Freire of the Brazilian army. The mission was initially to last three months, incorporating ten officers and one doctor from each guarantor country. Four Blackhawk U.S. helicopters and one C-98 Brazilian aircraft provided support for the operation. On June 10, an extension of three months was decided upon, and on August 22, MOMEP II was created with a new definition of procedures. The initial separation of forces occurred in March, but in August there were skirmishes between the Yaupi-Santiago border mark and the Cusumaza-Bambuiza border mark, and a renewed effort was necessary to achieve the separation of forces. In September, an extension of the area under the responsibility of MOMEP was established (security zone alpha), northeast of the demilitarized zone, where the parties could maintain military posts under the control of the mission.

The Itamaraty Declaration and a further document referring more specifically to the procedures to be undertaken by the mission set out four stages for the operation: the preparatory stage, the supervision of a cease-fire, the separation of forces, and demilitarization and demobilization. In May, in accordance with stage four, the mission presented a demobilization plan clearly defining timetables and troop movements.

On August 1, after negotiations had taken place in June and July, a demilitarized zone of 528 kilometers entered into effect. The dispute on the definition of the demilitarized zone stemmed from a divergence on the inclusion or exclusion of Banderas, the issue having been negotiated by the deputy foreign ministers of the parties. Support was lacking within Ecuador for the inclusion of Banderas in the demilitarized zone, while Peru requested reassurances regarding the use of the post. In fact, final agreement on the definition of the demilitarized zone was reached in July, just in time for U.S. defense secretary William Perry to announce it at the Williamsburg Defense Ministerial Meeting as an example of regional cooperation on security issues, a theme discussed during that gathering.

Several incidents took place between 1995 and 1998. The Ecuadorian base of Banderas and the Peruvian post PV-2 violated the terms of the initial agreement, which determined the boundaries of the demilitarized zone, and action was taken by the mission. In July 1998, Ecuadorian and Peruvian forces intensified their action on the border and again a separation of forces was necessary, a "zone of control" having been created just south of the demilitarized zone. The mission remained throughout its deployment an observation mission and did not undertake responsibilities that would lead to the use of force. In order to maintain impartiality, the headquarters were moved between Bagua, in Peru, and Patuca, in Ecuador, each week. In addition to the functions described above, the mission helped to demarcate the border and to remove mines from the area, a task made more difficult by the lack of proper information on their location.

Several decisions favored the development of greater confidence in the area of the conflict. The visits by military leaders of the guarantor countries; the adoption of a Cartilla de Seguridad, which standardized procedures for patrol encounters; the incorporation of Peruvian and Ecuadorian officers to the observer force; crossborder visits by military commanders; and the organization of athletic events[46] were relevant mechanisms that tackled the sensitive issue of relations between both military establishments and units on the ground. Furthermore, the Superior Consultative Committee of the mission, which met periodically at the Brazilian Embassies in Quito and Lima or at the Brazilian army headquarters in Brasilia, incorporated liaison officers from both Peru and Ecuador.

The mission remained in the area for four and a half years. In fact, it ceased its activities in June 1999, nine months after a final agreement was reached, the demarcation of the border having been concluded on May 12, 1999. The mission controlled the zone of conflict during this period, fulfilling its mandate. More importantly, during 1996, 1997, and the first half of 1998, it insulated the mediation process from localized military confrontation in the Cenepa region.

THE LATIN AMERICAN SECURITY CONTEXT

The security environment will be considered here, as outlined in the introduction to this research, in terms of the ideational and cultural factors that constitute it. According to Ronald Jepperson, Alexander Wendt, and Peter Katzenstein, institutions, norms, and patterns of amity and enmity are the three layers in which national security policies are made.[47] In this case, we would like to highlight two norms that mark the Latin American security environment: conflict resolution by peaceful means and noninterventionism. The idea that peace is a regional asset also became a prevailing value in the 1990s.

Latin America is one of the most peaceful regions of the world; one must not, however, ignore the history of conflict in the area. Boundary disputes were a reality throughout the history of the region, guerrilla warfare can be found in abundance from the late 1950s onward, power struggles between major players have generated great tension, and currently narcotraffic has become a central security threat. Although, when compared to other parts of the world, the number of deaths in battle or the rate of expenditure on arms acquisitions in the region is small, sources of tension and violent interstate clashes were quite significant until the 1990s. Major wars occurred in the nineteenth century, and U.S. interventions mark the history of the continent, especially before the 1930s. Looking back on the twentieth century, observers may be struck by the Chaco War (1932–1935), by the massacre of Haitian peasants by the Dominican military (1937), by the conflicts between Peru and Ecuador (1942, 1981, 1995), by the "soccer" war between Honduras and El Salvador (1969), by the conflict in Central America (1980s), by the Malvinas/Falklands War (1982), by the regional repercussions of the Cold War, and by a great number of U.S.-led interventions that distinguish regional international relations.

Interstate conflict or tension in Latin America has occurred as a result of the power struggle between regional players, the persistent interests of world powers, the overflow of domestic conflict, disagreements over the definition of boundaries inherited from colonial disputes or the unfinished demarcation process of the nineteenth century, and, more recently, as a result of narcotraffic. At the same time, multilateral efforts to tackle such sources of conflict can be found throughout the twentieth century and even earlier—for example the Panama Congress of countries that had just won independence from Spain in 1826. In that instance, two principles guided the treaty reached by the new republics: the peaceful solution of conflict and noninterference in domestic affairs. During the twentieth century, the norm of peaceful resolution of conflict developed slowly, incorporating the United States and Brazil.

In the Western Hemisphere there is a century-old tradition of attempts at concerted action in the security sphere. The OAS is among regional, multilateral organizations, including the Organization of African Unity and the Arab League, that have a clear mandate to intervene in disputes. The idea of a multilateral stance on hemispheric security began to be shaped during the mid-1930s. At the Buenos Aires Conference in 1936, delegates adopted the Convention for the Maintenance, Preservation, and Re-establishment of Peace. The Lima Inter-American Conference, which took place in 1938 in the context of mounting tension in Europe, issued the Declaration of Lima, stating the principle of common defense, and established the Consultative Meeting of Ministers of Foreign Affairs to consider emergency security matters. This was the first move since the end of the nineteenth century to include a security agenda in the multilateral arrangements in place in the hemisphere.[48] The security structure for the next half century was put in place during World War II. The Declaration of Reciprocal Assistance and Cooperation for the Defense of the Americas was adopted, stating clearly that an attack on one American state would be considered an attack on all, and the Inter-American Defense Board, composed of military and naval advisers from member states, was created.

As the end of the World War II approached, the institutionalization of the inter-American system took root.[49] At the Chapultepec Conference, held in 1945, three basic documents were drafted: a treaty of reciprocal assistance, a basic constitution for a regional organization, and a treaty to coordinate and consolidate agreement on the pacific settlement of disputes.[50] At this conference, aggressions perpetuated by American states themselves were considered under the banner of mutual security. During the Rio de Janeiro Conference, held in 1947, the Inter-American Treaty of Reciprocal Assistance was signed. The following year, at the Bogotá Conference, the Charter of the Organization of American States, the Inter-American Treaty on Pacific Settlement (Pact of Bogotá), and the American Declaration on the Rights and Duties of Man were issued. Article 26 of the OAS charter refers to a special treaty that should establish mechanisms for the settlement of disputes: the Pact of Bogotá fulfills this commitment.

The charter of the OAS provided for the Meeting of Ministers of Foreign Affairs to be one of the main organs of the organization.[51] Ministers were to consult on threats to hemispheric peace, dispute settlement, and resistance of external attacks, and were to be assisted by the Advisory Defense Committee, composed of high-ranking military officers of member states. The Council of the Organization, composed of ambassadorial representatives from each country, could act provisionally as the consultative organ when hemispheric security was threatened. In 1962, the special consultative Committee on Security was created. In October during that same year, the Inter-American Defense College opened in Washington.

The 1967 Protocol of Buenos Aires, which amended the 1948 charter, created the Permanent Council (which succeeded the Council of the Organization of American States), establishing that its basic role would be that of peacekeeping and mediation, handling matters referred to it by the General Assembly or the Meeting of Ministers of Foreign Affairs. At this point, the Inter-American Committee on Peaceful Settlement was created as a subsidiary body, assisting the Permanent Council and replacing the Inter-American Peace Committee. The creation of these institutions was accompanied by a tendency to deal with border conflicts by referring them to these or other international mechanisms.

The prospects for concerted action in the sphere of security are hindered in the Western Hemisphere by the noninterventionist tradition, strongly rooted in Latin American political culture. U.S. interventions in the Caribbean, the Monroe Doctrine of 1823, and the Roosevelt Corollary, enunciated in 1904, generated sustained concern among Latin Americans regarding U.S. interventionist policies. Based on a prior tradition, expressed in the Calvo and Drago doctrines, which stresses territorial sovereignty and nonintervention, one of the basic principles of the inter-American system became noninterventionism.[52] At the Montevideo Conference in 1933, the Convention on the Right and Duties of States was adopted, enshrining the principle of nonintervention in the inter-American system. The principle is present in the Protocol Relative to Non-Intervention signed at the Buenos Aires Conference in 1936 and has been incorporated into other treaties, most notably the OAS Charter (Articles 18–22, 15–20).

Only in 1991, most Latin America countries having adopted democratic governments, was it possible to issue the Declaration of Santiago, which foresees measures in the case of the interruption of democratic government. Nevertheless, the prevalence of the principle of nonintervention over ideas of defense of human rights and democracy impeded the implementation of multilateral measures when cases were reported of violation of human rights and disrespect for the democratic principles enshrined in the OAS Charter. Even after the adoption of the Declaration of Santiago by the OAS General

Assembly, the crises in Haiti in 1991 and in Peru in 1992 were met with a weak response.

In this context, despite a long tradition of institution building, the collective security and conflict resolution mechanisms available were not put to work to solve disputes that could clearly turn into crises or violent confrontation. A pattern was established of reactive behavior toward crises.[53] Nonetheless, the institution-building history, allied to the hemisphere's legalist tradition, provided a frame in which a norm of peaceful conflict resolution could be set. The noninterventionist tradition, despite having hindered the development of a stronger collective security system, is closely associated with the norm of peaceful conflict resolution in Latin America: it is associated with wide support for a legalist international order that would protect the region from great power interventionism.

The inter-American system was severely hit by its failure to deal with the crisis over the Malvinas/Falkland Islands after Argentina invaded the area and British forces penetrated the hemispheric security zone defined in the Rio treaty,[54] and also by the Central American crisis. The United States made unilateral decisions to intervene both in Grenada in 1983 and in Panama in 1989. The role played by ad hoc coalitions became increasingly relevant, particularly in the context of the Central American crisis. The Contadora Group and Contadora Support Group and later the Rio Group are potentially valuable informal mechanisms of political coordination and conflict resolution that can, in the context of diplomatic negotiations, allow for the continuing construction of the norm of peaceful conflict resolution.[55]

Mediation, in particular, has been common practice in Latin America, embedded in a wider culture of peaceful conflict resolution. The Pact of Bogotá (Article IX) predicts the use of this mechanism, and the Inter-American Peace Committee has been used by the OAS. Some cases were successful, such as the pope's 1978 offer of the services of Cardinal Antonio Samoré as mediator between Chile and Argentina and the mediation of the Central American crisis. Others were blunt failures, such as the attempt to mediate the Argentine–United Kingdom conflict prior to the Malvinas/Falklands War.

In contrast to the two previous decades, when there was an upturn in violent clashes in Latin America, the 1990s can be characterized as a period when a perception became widespread that it was important to preserve the image of Latin America as a peaceful region where, despite economic and social problems, interstate violence could be successfully avoided. This view is clearly stated by Chilean academic Augusto Varas:

> The main change that has occurred in hemispheric security since the Cold War is its new center of gravity. In contrast to the past, when it centered around extra continental threats, the security of the hemisphere's nations must be based upon a different challenge. Currently, this challenge is none other than to create the best conditions for establishing effective, efficient mechanisms and institutions to achieve sustainable hemispheric peace. Hemispheric security must be organized around defending the principal collective good of the hemisphere's community of nations. And these nations, increasingly integrated at the level of trade and the economy, have to protect their main collective good: hemispheric peace.[56]

The transition toward democratic regimes in most countries, the adoption of neoliberal economic policies, and the end of the Cold War constituted the background to this shifting center of gravity. A number of long-standing disputes were effectively tackled during this period.[57] The Miami Presidential Summit of December 11, 1994, and the July 25, 1995, meeting of Defense Ministers of the Americas in Williamsburg, Virginia, confirmed that peace and stability were being treated as regional assets.

By the end of the 1980s, the Esquipulas II Accords were in place, and the OAS and the UN were involved in a continuous effort to deal with the complex problems of the Central American countries.[58] In February 1990, the United Kingdom and Argentina reestablished diplomatic relations, although their main dispute had not been resolved. In April 1990, Venezuela and Trinidad and Tobago signed a treaty to settle their dispute over jurisdiction in the Gulf of Paria waters. On September 6, 1991, the conflict between Belize and Guatemala, which dates back to British colonial rule of British Honduras, took a new direction, with the recognition of Belize as a sovereign state by President Jorge Serrano and the initiation of diplomatic relations. The World Court adjudicated the final demarcation of the land and sea boundary between Honduras and El Salvador, and the settlement was implemented.

In South America, the relationship between the subregional powers changed dramatically. Brazil and Argentina signed the nuclear safeguard agreement, redeploying away from battle readiness at their border; they also established exchanges of military information and personnel and participated in joint military exercises. After dealing with their territorial disputes, cooperation became a possibility in relations between Argentina and Chile: they reached agreement over the Southern Ice Fields during the same year in which Peru and Ecuador settled their differences.

By 1993, in the sphere of disarmament, the Tlatelolco Treaty of 1967 had been endorsed by all Latin American countries, and the quadripartite nuclear safeguards agreement has been in force since 1994.[59] That year, Argentina adopted its Nuclear Non-Proliferation Treaty, and Brazil followed suit in 1998. In 1991, Bolivia, Colombia, Ecuador, Peru, and Venezuela signed the Cartagena Declaration renouncing the possession, production, development, use, or transfer of all weapons of mass destruction; Argentina, Brazil, and Chile also signed the Mendoza Commitment, which prohibits the production, development, warehousing, or transfer of chemical or biological weapons.

At the same time, attempts were being made to revive the role of the OAS in the security sphere, in line with a trend in the United Nations favoring greater cooperation with regional organizations.[60] In this context, the norm of peaceful conflict resolution found a new institutional backing and was redefined in terms of the concept of cooperative security.

During the 1991 Santiago meeting, a resolution titled "Cooperation for Hemispheric Security" was issued, and a Commitment to Democracy and the Renewal of the Inter-American System was approved by the OAS General Assembly. The following year, the Special Committee on Hemispheric Security was created, with a mandate to deal with conflict prevention and conflict management and to study the security needs of small states in the hemisphere. The organization was effectively shifting its focus from collective security to cooperative security. Emphasis on deterrence based on the principle that aggressors would have to face the combined force of a coalition was replaced by emphasis on confidence-building measures that guaranteed the transparency of military procedures and the availability of information.[61] The exchange of information between neighboring countries, mutual visits, and participation in joint activities have steadily increased.[62] In 1995, a regional conference on confidence-building measures was held in Chile, and in 1998 another took place in San Salvador. Furthermore, the countries in the region inform the UN of their defense-sector allocations. The Rio Group has also discussed peaceful settlement mechanisms throughout the decade, although it has generated very little concerted action.

U.S. government support for such changes is, of course, fundamental. Taking the view that narcotraffic, arms dealing, and other transnational criminal actions are the main threats in the hemisphere and that maintaining open-market economies and democratic regimes is a core objective, the Clinton administration favored multilateral activity and confidence-building measures.[63]

The changing relation between the military and civil authorities in most countries should also be borne in mind. The transition to democracy was accompanied by greater control of the military establishment by civil authorities, although the process is neither homogeneous nor stabilized in all locations. The role of multilateral efforts in the sphere of collective security, cooperative security, and peace operations is discussed domestically in diplomatic, academic, and military circles.

One additional aspect of the regional security environment to be considered is Brazil's role and position. During the 1990s the Brazilian decisionmaking elite pursued a foreign policy distinguished by a strong drive toward conformity with international norms and rules. Elected governments would pursue a *strategy of insertion,*[64] a concept embracing the acceptance of international regimes, increased participation in UN operations, and an emphasis on regional stability rather than subregional competition. The Brazilian government has largely backed and contributed to establishing the image of a region characterized by peace and stability. This can be seen most clearly in Brazil's policies toward its neighbor and former rival, Argentina.

On the other hand, specific concerns regarding the Amazon region warrant investigation. The most obvious changes in Brazil's definition of its security policy since the 1980s are a result of the new context of its relationship with Argentina and the priority given to new aspects of regional security, such as drug traffic and the control over the Amazon Basin. Sovereignty over the Amazon River Basin is a central preoccupation of military strategists. During the mid-1980s, the armed forces installed an unsuccessful program, Calha Norte, that sought to expand the military presence in the area. The Amazonian Watch System (SIVAM), now in place, is a communication and monitoring system that aims to control the flow of drugs, of illegal commerce, and of environmental resources, and to protect indigenous populations.

While the end of the Cold War had a significant impact on the security environment in Central America and the Caribbean, the effect of systemic changes in the late 1980s and 1990s in South America is less clear. Global trends in the wider redefinition of the concept of security did have an important, although fragmented, influence on elite perceptions.[65] Problems such as border disputes and narcotraffic, however, must be considered in their own right. The 1995 war between Peru and Ecuador and the tension between Venezuela and Colombia in Lake Maracaibo made this reality patent.

The Cenepa War and the negotiations that followed should be understood in the context of a regional security environment that, during the 1990s, was in the process of reconstructing the norm of peaceful conflict resolution in terms of changing foreign policies, restructuring regional institutions, and treating peace as an asset. At the same time, the norm of nonintervention brought the limits and features of the multilateral endeavor into focus.

DOMESTIC CONDITIONS IN ECUADOR AND PERU

Most Latin American economists agree that the 1980s were, with a few exceptions such as Chile, the lost decade for the continent's economies. The debt crisis produced chronic balance-of-payment deficits and fiscal problems resulting in high inflation rates and a steady decline in economic growth. Efforts to increase exports in order to service the debt were insufficient, and the capacity to acquire new loans was compromised by growing uncertainty about the countries' ability to honor their commitments in the future. In fact, after the Mexican moratorium of 1982, financial flows to Latin America were drastically reduced and conditioned to the adoption of policies of austerity monitored by the IMF. Overall, the diagnosis that the import substitution model of development, guided by the state, was reaching exhaustion gradually prevailed within multilateral agencies and among the policymaking and entrepreneurial elite.

The story of the neoliberal shift in Latin American economies has been extensively analyzed and will not be reproduced here. For the purposes of this research, it is sufficient to say that Peru and

Ecuador were not spared from the economic turbulence of the 1980s and that both countries were forced to undertake, although with varying degrees of intensity, adjustment policies under the supervision of the IMF that had considerable impact on both states' economic roles and the usual negative effects on their ability to address social problems such as poverty, low standards of education, highly insufficient health systems, and unemployment.

Economic crises, associated with worsening social conditions, put considerable pressure on governments born out of democratic transition from authoritarian rule in the 1970s. While these new democratic rulers enjoyed the legitimacy granted by their popular mandates and by the high value attached to the reconstruction of democratic institutions by the majority of society, by the end of the decade economic deterioration inevitably took its toll. In Peru, Alan Garcia's government ended, bearing the blame for a dismal economic record and under accusations of mismanagement and corruption that produced widespread skepticism toward the political system and democratic institutions. The election of Alberto Fujimori in 1990 should be interpreted in the light of the dramatic downfall of the Garcia government. He was an outsider, who criticized the traditional political establishment and promised bold economic reforms inspired by neoliberal theory.

In Ecuador, the first democratically elected government after military rule came to power in 1980 when the economic environment had not yet wholly deteriorated, enabling Jaime Roldos to adopt a center-left economic program and a rather independent and progressive foreign policy.[66] President Roldos died tragically in a plane accident in 1981 and was replaced by his vice president, Osvaldo Hurtado, a Christian Democrat much more inclined to market reforms and less bold in his foreign policy. According to Hey, economic policies in Ecuador began to show a "trend towards neoliberalism" following the crisis of 1982, despite the different inclinations of the successive administrations. In this sense, it is fair to say that economic reforms in Ecuador started earlier than in Peru, even though the pace, depth, and outcomes of these processes varied considerably. In Peru, for instance, the neoliberal "revolution" was implemented through President Fujimori's shock policies in a context of political radicalization and disruption of democratic institutions. In Ecuador, reforms seem to have been gradual and at times tentative, culminating with the more dramatic measures taken by

President Mahuad (1998–2000) when the economy was in disarray. The main differences between the two pathways regard the extent of their liberalizing reforms and their respective consequences for democratic order. Overall, however, Peru and Ecuador have followed economic strategies common to most Latin American countries during the 1990s in their search for the redefinition of their place in the new international order. Although these strategies do not, as Hey has noted in the case of Ecuador, necessarily produce a convergence between economic and foreign policies, they do reflect a historical shift from the dominant paradigm that had previously oriented development policies—a paradigm upon which the very constitution of the modern state in the subcontinent was based. Neoliberal reforms are not confined to changes in economic policy. They have led to reforms of the state in a wide range of areas, from the withdrawal of public participation in productive activities to the privatization of services and social security programs. State reform has had a considerable impact on traditional political alignments that sustained the ruling elite for long periods of time, in civil as well as military governments in Latin America. In Peru, the entire party system was delegitimized under Fujimori because it proved incapable of implementing urgently needed reforms. In Ecuador, the political instability that plagued the country in the 1990s also reflects the tensions between the shortcomings of policies that have failed to redress the economy and lack the support of important sectors of the political elite. Be that as it may, the broader process of economic globalization has forced the redefinition of interests and ideas about the direction of development strategies, which are now geared predominantly toward negotiating the "internationalization" of domestic economies previously protected by the state from external competition.

The international relations of Latin American countries, then, have entered a phase of gradual realignment that, in very general terms, favors deeper integration within a regional and world order shaped by a liberal democratic ideal associated with the United States. These changes in the international environment did not produce clear-cut shifts in the foreign policies of Peru and Ecuador during the post–Cold War period, either toward the United States or in their bilateral relations. Yet it is our contention that, at the time of the negotiations to settle the territorial dispute, both the perceptions and interests of influential social and political actors in Peru and Ecuador and the perceptions of policymakers on both sides were increasingly sensitive to the imperatives of a global order that imposed heavy costs on countries involved in armed conflicts that threatened regional stability and affected negatively the investment environment of these countries. Moreover, the conflict occurred in a continent that not only had a peaceful record but was also the object of ambitious plans to form a hemispheric free trade area under North American leadership.

It is important to stress, however, that the building of neoliberal consensus was not devoid of contradictions and imposed considerable social and political costs on these societies. Additionally, this consensus did not necessarily establish conditions conducive to the peaceful settlement of the conflict. In the final analysis, Peru and Ecuador were involved in processes of redefinition of interests and identities that reduced the relevance of the territorial issue that had driven their rivalry for decades, vis-à-vis the goal of integration with the global political economy.

The literature consulted and the interviews conducted during our research tend to support this hypothesis, but they also reveal relevant differences between the domestic contexts in both countries. In Ecuador, market-oriented reforms were being implemented in the 1980s, particularly during the presidency of Leon Febres Cordero (1984–1988), a center-right politician and businessman who favored closer ties to the United States and little commitment to multilateral diplomacy efforts such as the Andean Pact. Febres Cordero took no initiative toward reopening negotiations over the territorial problem with Peru. In fact, during the negotiations that led to the 1998 agreement, the former president expressed his staunch opposition to its terms. It was not until the presidency of the socialist Rodrigo Borja (1988–1992) that the border issue received the full attention of the Ecuadorian diplomacy, with the proposal for arbitration of the issue by the pope.[67] This initiative was part of a more proactive foreign policy that valued participation in multilateral organizations.

At the same time, the newly elected President Fujimori expressed his intention of adopting a foreign policy aimed at resolving old grievances with regional neighbors such as Chile and Ecuador in an effort to reinforce his policy of economic openness to international investors. The rapprochement between the two countries led to the Peruvian president's historic visit to Quito in January 1992, and talks aimed at opening negotiations to deal with the territorial problem. At the time, Fujimori's reforms were already underway, with lower inflation rates and some economic growth, but were facing strong opposition in congress. The April 1992 *autogolpe* removed such opposition, paved the way for the radicalization of neoliberal reforms, and gave the military a freer hand to combat the guerillas of the Sendero Luminoso. The coup drew sharp criticism from the international community and led to Peru's relative isolation in multilateral forums.

Negotiations with Ecuador were affected because the Peruvian president missed important occasions when talks were scheduled to take place—Peru was suspended from the Rio Group, Fujimori did not attend the meeting of the Andean Pact due to hostility from Venezuela, and the planned meeting at the Ibero-American Summit in Madrid was canceled since the Peruvian president decided to leave early because of the cold reception he was given. Moreover, Foreign Minister Blacker Miller, who had been heading negotiations with Ecuador, was replaced by a military officer, indicating that policy regarding the territorial issue was under the scrutiny, and now greater control, of the armed forces. As a result, talks were frozen, and there was a void in bilateral negotiations until the 1995 conflict erupted.

Meanwhile in Ecuador the new president, Sixto Duran Ballén, took office in August 1992, and did little to follow up his predecessor's foreign policy. In Hey's evaluation, Ballén was noteworthy for his "lack of activity in the political/diplomatic arena," but was responsible for stepping up neoliberal programs and for a further alignment with the United States. His tenure coincided with the height of "Fujipopulism," the infamous combination of authoritarian politics, populism, and orthodox economic policies that drew praise for Peru from many international investors and financial agencies, and criticism from human rights groups worldwide.[68]

Though, at the beginning of his mandate, Fujimori forged a foreign policy that would contribute to Peru's new approach to international markets and build support for his reforms, after the authoritarian developments of 1992 his rule became increasingly dependent on the support of the military, who not only acquired a central role in the repression of the guerrilla movement and the management of the intelligence and security apparatus but, in the process, became ever more politicized. Also, once the more "flexible" foreign policy approach was abandoned, traditional positions regarding the territorial issue with Ecuador, still dominant in the Peruvian foreign office, once again set the tone. As we have suggested in the previous chapter, the failure to implement the 1991 agreements on confidence measures at the border contributed to the heightening of tensions that led to the 1995 war. In Ecuador, President Ballén's apathy left the matter under the direct responsibility of the military, effectively marginalizing diplomatic channels in the moment of crisis.

We can say, then, that in Peru the domestic context that preceded the war was characterized by a combination of authoritarianism, deepening neoliberal reforms, an increased military involvement in politics and in administering the apparatus of repression, and a foreign policy at pains to overcome the isolation produced by the coup of 1992. In Ecuador, on the other hand, democratic rule was relatively stable, but the military held considerable autonomy in defense matters—particularly on the border issue; neoliberal reforms continued at a faster pace; and foreign policy assumed a low profile, in which the initiative undertaken by the Borja administration to reopen negotiations with Peru was abandoned.

In 1995, both presidents were finishing their terms. Fujimori was running for re-election in the April ballot; the Ecuadorian president was not up for a second term. Some Ecuadorian analysts interviewed emphasized the Peruvian president's re-election campaign as an explanatory factor for the war. There is no conclusive evidence to link the campaign to the outbreak of the hostilities in the Cenepa. Fujimori's victory was probable in January 1995, though by no means certain. In fact, in April he won with 64 percent of the valid votes but just 52 percent of the overall vote, largely thanks to successful tactics to divide the opposition and widespread use of the machinery of government—including the military—to boost his popularity.[69] It is unlikely, though, that electoral strategy would warrant the undertaking of such a risky and unpredictable enterprise as war. If anything, the war was more of an embarrassment to the Peruvian government, because the initial setbacks and casualties brought into public view the unpreparedness of the Peruvian military to fight a war in the Amazon region. In Ecuador, on the other hand, the war greatly increased the military's prestige in public opinion, and the government's management of the conflict—largely controlled by the military itself—received a very positive evaluation.

Between 1995 and 1998—the years of negotiation—Peru and Ecuador faced quite different domestic scenarios that affected, in various degrees, the pace and perspectives of the peace talks. It is surprising that the process did not suffer any serious interruption given the serious political instability in Ecuador during those years. President Abdalá Bucaran replaced President Ballén in August 1996 and was deposed by congress for "reasons of insanity" in February 1997. After a period of institutional crisis during which Congress debated who should replace the ousted ruler, the military exercised considerable leverage in determining the final outcome, supporting the claim of the chairman of congress, Fabian Alarcon, to occupy the presidency rather than the vice president, given an alleged omission in the constitution on the matter. Alarcon stayed in power until August 1998, when the new elected president, Jamil Mahuad, took office.[70] Overall, Ecuador had four presidents during the three years from the end of the Cenepa War to the signature of the final agreements in Brasilia. Each had a different style in pursuing the negotiation process that to some degree influenced its pace. The important point here, however, is the striking continuity of Ecuador's general disposition to come to terms with the problem and sign a definitive peace in a context ripe with opportunities to use the conflict with Peru for political purposes. Bucaran, for instance, who was known for the unorthodox personal style that had earned him the nickname El Loco, could very well have changed the direction of the negotiations to gather internal support when his government's legitimacy was seriously challenged. Instead, he accepted President Fujimori's invitation and, in January 1997, became the first Ecuadorian head of state to visit Peru, a month before he was deposed. His behavior was criticized by many in Ecuador for being too conciliatory toward the Peruvians. In fact, after taking office in 1996, President Bucaran kept the same negotiating team and retained foreign minister Galo Leoro. Under President Alarcon, the Ecuadorian delegation to the talks in Brasilia was also retained almost without changes, and the new foreign minister, Jose Ayala, a career diplomat serving at the UN, proved an able negotiator, committed to the conclusion of the process.[71] Finally, President Mahuad, who took office in August 1998 when the negotiations were at a crucial juncture, had, as we argue in other sections of this chapter, an important role in concluding the accords: he confirmed Ayala as chancellor, reaffirming the continuity and consolidation of the country's policy.

The continuity in Ecuador's policy toward the border issue is remarkable given the difficult political and economic conditions in the country during the negotiating period. The armed forces' performance in the Cenepa War had enhanced the military's prestige in the political arena; their role in the crisis that led to the removal of Presidents Bucaran and Mahuad confirmed it. Nevertheless, the "internationalization" of the negotiation and mediation process had removed the main levers of control from their hands. Once Ecuador decided to accept that negotiations would be conducted under the aegis of the Rio Protocol, the degree of control by domestic players was substantially reduced. That may be the reason why important actors such as General Francisco Paco Moncayo, a war hero and later mayor of Quito, voiced his strong opposition to the acceptance of the protocol's framework.[72]

Another important consequence of the war was to "restore the country's honor" following long decades of perceived humiliation after the defeat of 1941, in society at large but especially among the new generation of military officers who took part in the Cenepa War and among those who still remembered vividly the dramatic events of the past.

The war also generated—if not immediately, at least during the three years of the process—a general feeling favorable to a definitive settlement. Public opinion polls registered majority support for the conclusion of the accords; more importantly, the press and the business community played a crucial role in defending the peace. Ecuadorian press reports on the mediation process were mostly positive, and the government's handling of public opinion relied more on transparency than on secrecy, a sign that the officials in charge recognized that the final agreement depended on a successful effort to convince Ecuadorian society that the peace would benefit the country, even though the outcome might not fulfill the historic aspirations that most citizens as schoolchildren had learned were legitimate claims attached to the national identity.

The business community, on the other hand, favored an agreement based on the perception that peace was indispensable for the recovery of the country's economy, either because it would benefit from promised funds from multilateral agencies to finance bilateral integration or because broader plans for regional integration were at stake. Francisco Huerta, who participated in the negotiating team on confidence-building measures and was later a chief cabinet minister in Gustavo Noboa's government, defined the months and weeks that preceded the conclusion of the treaties as dominated by a strict "economic logic" that practically pegged a price to peace itself. This perspective, which predominated among the entrepreneurial class on the coast as well as in the highlands, became increasingly influential among the press. Former chancellor Cordovez criticized this approach as "peace at any price."[73] One might even say peace at a very particular price.

The perception that the economic crisis in Ecuador was a strong incentive to peace was also present among Peruvian negotiators. Eduardo Ponce, one of the leading members of the delegation and later ambassador to Brazil, stated that he always "noticed that among the Ecuadorian entrepreneurial milieu the territorial issue was transcended . . . and that the resolution of the problems was important for the Ecuadorian regional position."[74]

Finally, it is no less important to stress the mobilization of several groups in Ecuadorian civil society to discuss the conflict and elaborate proposals for the negotiation process. Academics, businessmen, nongovernmental organizations, the church, and other sectors of society took part in a national debate that was probably vital to the construction of a consensus for peace. More specifically, the participation of a significant group of intellectuals, journalists, and leaders in social movements from both countries in conferences organized in Peru, Ecuador, and at the University of Maryland to discuss possible negotiation strategies was certainly significant in involving civil society actors from both countries in the process.[75]

The negotiations occurred during the first years of President Fujimori's second term, in a Peruvian environment that contrasted sharply with the instability of Ecuadorian politics. Fujimori had been involved in the solution of the border problem with Ecuador since the beginning of his first mandate, when he had to deal with the 1991 crisis and respond to the Borja proposal for papal arbitration. He was also the signatory of the Brasilia Accords in 1998. This continuity in leadership does not, however, warrant the conclusion that the Peruvian policy maintained throughout a steady course. Indeed, we have seen that in 1991 Fujimori was more inclined to a flexible political negotiation with Ecuador; after the April 1992 coup, his diplomacy receded into a more rigid defense of the traditional position of implementing the Rio Protocol. The war in 1995 generated tensions among sectors of the military who were unhappy about the lack of logistical support in the first days of the war and about the losses of several aircraft in battle. A climate of revenge grew in the armed forces that lingered during the years of negotiation and put talks at risk during the July 1998 crisis. Fujimori's relation with the military thus changed gradually during his second term, a result of the inevitable divisions produced by the involvement of the armed forces in the political administration of the state, and, as recent evidence has shown, of the influence of his close adviser for national security, Vladimiro Montesinos, who apparently manipulated the acquisition of military equipment, including the notorious Mig-29s and SU-25s, in order to fuel a corruption scheme that involved much of the political and military elite in Peru. The war also produced some public resentment regarding the preparedness of the army to defend its borders. However, Fujimori's grip over the media and his deployment of the intelligence apparatus to repress more critical antigovernment expressions insulated the debate about the border conflict from public opinion to a considerable degree.[76] In this sense, the more authoritarian complexion of Peruvian politics from 1995 to 1998 contrasted with the Ecuadorian government's effort to build a consensus around an honorable agreement, despite the country's political and economic instability.

Some analysts would credit the Peruvian president's insulation of negotiations from governmental and societal criticism with strengthening the "presidential diplomacy" that contributed to the advancement of the process at critical and decisive junctures. Former minister Francisco Tudela attributed to the president's determined support his successful bid to convince the Peruvian government and congress to accept the Santiago agreements that established the framework for negotiations based on the Rio Protocol.[77] The kidnapping of Tudela and other diplomats and government officials at the Japanese Embassy in December 1996 created a political crisis that would last for months and undoubtedly stalled the pace of the negotiation process. Tudela had played an important role in overcoming the more conservative sectors in the Peruvian foreign office, and his absence was felt at the first meetings in Brasilia in 1997. He was subsequently replaced by Eduardo Ferrero, a comparative hardliner, who adopted a more rigid stance regarding any possible concessions based on political criteria that skirted the legal framework of the protocol. His opposition to the Tiwintza formula, arbitrated by the guarantor countries in 1998, led to his resignation shortly before the signature of the final accords.

The oscillation in the foreign office indicated that Fujimori faced resistance inside the government to an agreement that included the recognition of some of the basic Ecuadorian claims. In 1998,

Fujimori was involved in a political battle to reform the constitution to allow his re-election to a third term. As it had not in 1992 and 1995, the conclusion of the peace appeared an important factor in his chances of success. The political domestic context would thus explain the centralization of negotiations around the presidency, particularly in the decisive months of 1998 when the process was at risk. Fujimori strongly believed his political interests would be served by the conclusion of the peace and was bold enough to remove the powerful head of the armed forces, General Hermosa, when he proposed the use of force to counter the Ecuadorian army's alleged penetration into sectors of the demilitarized zone. Finally, it is important to note that despite the Peruvian president's ability to control the main elements of the negotiation, he did not have the same margins of liberty to make concessions to Ecuador because he was constrained by the agreements that had been reached at various junctures of the Itamaraty process. In other words, the Peruvian success in framing the outcome according to the letter of the Rio Protocol limited the president's options when a more political solution became necessary.

CONCEPTS AND METHODS OF THE MEDIATION PROCESS

Of the conflict-management mechanisms the international system has generated, in this instance mediation was the path chosen. Active participation in the negotiating process by the guarantors was observed, the suggestions and proposals made were not binding, and consent by the parties was reached.[78] As noted earlier, this mechanism is likely to be used in cases involving a long drawn-out and complex dispute.[79] Moreover, this particular mediation process was geared toward conflict resolution, not conflict management as earlier attempts to solve the Peru-Ecuador dispute had been.

Given the level of institutionalization and the role played by the formal proposals made by the mediators, this particular process could be defined as a conciliation.[80] This is also a mechanism envisaged in the 1948 Pact of Bogotá and was used in the case of the constitution of the Chaco Conciliation Commission in 1929.[81] Since, however, the concept of *conciliation* was not used by the actors and a conciliation commission was not formally constituted, we shall not apply the term. Nevertheless, it allows one to perceive the relevance of the legal documents that framed the negotiation and the increasing relevance during the process of the proposals formally presented by the mediators.

The concept of guarantors, present in the 1942 protocol, was imported from private law and is applied to international law indicating a guarantee that a contract will be respected. It should be understood in the context of a tendency to apply ad hoc devices after World War I, as a substitute for a strong collective security mechanism. It is a mechanism of stabilization but not, in itself, of negotiation.[82]

Arbitration also played a role in the settlement of this dispute, the parties having sought arbitration by the mediators in 1998. This mechanism had played a previous role in this particular conflict in the form of the Diaz de Aguiar Award and had been suggested several times as a possible solution to the controversy. Furthermore, the mechanism has a wider presence in the region, having been used on other occasions, also constituting a part of the procedures envisaged in the Pact of Bogotá.

Both parties agreed on the states that would fulfill the role of guarantors, having actively sought the mediation of the four states involved. This was true despite the disputed status of the 1942 protocol expressed, for instance, in Ecuador's use of the term *friend* in place of *guarantor*. After Chile, Argentina, Brazil, and the United States become actively involved (February 1995, Declaration by the Guarantors), we can refer to a process of international mediation by an ad hoc grouping. As we remarked earlier, the role played by ad hoc arrangements has been a recurrent feature of the Latin American security environment. In this case, the guarantors of the 1942 protocol became the mediators of the negotiation process. Since they were the guarantors of the agreement (Article 7 of the protocol), rather than a specific aspect of the bilateral relation such as the territorial boundary, their role as mediators stemmed from their responsibility for the implementation of the protocol.[83]

Motivations for the four guarantors of the 1942 protocol to get involved in the mediation process were manifest. First, a framework that called for the use of this mechanism was in place, thus a "mandate to intervene in the dispute" was available. Second, the ad hoc grouping had clear interests in controlling the dispute and ultimately finding a definite solution to it. The analysis of the Latin American context has shown that the concept of a peaceful and stable region, characterized by cooperative relations, became a hegemonic idea in the region and was treated as an asset. Moreover, the leadership in Brazil, Chile, Argentina, and the United States intensively promoted this concept during the period in question. As J. G. Merrills notes, the fact that the mediators see a settlement as furthering their own interests does not disqualify their participation.[84] In this case, the focus of the guarantors was the comprehensive settlement most clearly linked to the view of regional peace as an asset, not more particular interests. Third, the contending parties were interested in changing the nature of their relationship, albeit with significant limitations to the concessions they could and would like to make. The investigation of the domestic context has shown that in both countries there was an inclination toward a redefinition of bilateral relations.

The disputing parties, as we have seen, accepted the mediation mechanism as a measure that could reduce the risk of further conflict; "monitor, verify and guarantee" agreements reached; and serve as "a public expression of their commitment to genuine conflict management."[85] Thus, regardless of Ecuadorian objections to the 1942 protocol within the context of proposed changes to the original framework, it was not in Ecuador's interest to reject the role of the guarantors.

The role of the mediations allowed the leadership in both countries, but particularly in Ecuador, to share the cost of conflict resolution. The sharing of the political cost of compromise can be observed quite clearly at the last stages of the negotiation when, in fact, the parties requested that the guarantors become arbiters. In this instance, the mediators saved face for the authorities in both countries, particularly in Ecuador, where the leadership was weaker.[86]

The strategy adopted by the mediators involved a wide array of tactics. Since we are looking at a group of states, one can assume that the resources available were significant—but the motivation to invest in the negotiation process was even more important.

Communication-facilitation strategies, formulation strategies, and manipulation strategies were employed at different points in the mediation process.[87] In the first category, we are struck by the relevance of the identification of issues and interests that the mediators facilitated, particularly during the second phase of negotiations when procedures were established. The presentation of the list of "pending impasses" (presented on March 6, 1996) was identified as a central task, and its accomplishment opened the way for further talks.

In the second category, we would like to highlight the decision, made early in the process, to deal with simple issues first as well as the recommendation of procedures, in particular the division of the negotiations, into four subject groupings (Commissions I, II, III, IV, meeting in 1998). The incorporation of the principle of single undertaking, whereby all contending issues were to be settled jointly (rather than with the traditional technique of negotiation per item), and the decision not to allow further "impasses" to be added to the lists presented by each country were also made early in the negotiations. The role played by the mediators in the adoption of these procedures was fundamental.

Manipulation strategies were employed when substantive suggestions were made at two critical junctures. During the first phase of negotiations, the mediators facilitated the addition of four new documents to the negotiation framework, thus reconstructing the setting itself. In this case, the definition of the framework had direct implications for the substance of the negotiations, opening the door for the inclusion of important Ecuadorian grievances and tackling the long-standing dispute between the parties on the validity of the Rio Protocol. Moreover, in this manner the political line of argumentation and the juridical line of argumentation emphasized respectively by Ecuador and Peru were incorporated into the negotiation process. The same strategy was employed when the mediators made substantive proposals for the redefinition of bilateral relations in November 1997, and in each of the issue areas defined at the beginning of 1998. It is possible, here, to discern an increase in the mediators' intervention in the process, suggesting that their role becomes similar to that of conciliators, despite the informal nature of the proposals and the lack of a conciliation commission.

The mediators also worked hard on changing the parties' expectations, making it clear that Ecuadorian demands for borderline redefinition were unattainable and that, regardless of the balance of power between the two countries, Peru would have to deal with claims that were deeply rooted in Ecuador's national identity.

The pursuit of impartiality is a crucial factor in mediation processes. In this instance, the fact that the mediators were the original guarantors of a treaty rejected by one of the parties made this task even more difficult.[88] A review of the process indicates that, in this respect, the enlargement of the framework for negotiations was a crucial move. Ecuador had to accept the central status of the 1942 protocol, and Peru had to admit the inclusion of additional documents. The mediators had to show not only impartiality regarding the parties but also impartiality regarding the two forms of discourse stressed by the parties: that is, a discourse based on arguments of what is political and just and a discourse based on legality. This was successfully achieved by a constant, simultaneous emphasis on the juridical procedures and the necessity to accommodate political interests in order to achieve a definite and final solution to the problem. In the end, Peru would admit the incorporation of political arguments in order to guarantee the vindication of juridical arguments.

The timing of a mediation process is a crucial feature, leading in some cases to the derailing of the negotiations or to a resurgence of violent conflict. Two aspects demand particular consideration: taking advantage of a window of opportunity and the rhythm of negotiations. In the case analyzed here, two important moments were grasped by the mediators and by the contending parties themselves: the aftermath of the 1995 conflict and the power transition in Ecuador in 1998. In 1995, Ecuador having won a small victory in the Cenepa area and given the impact of an armed conflict in the Andes within the regional security environment outlined earlier, there was a window of opportunity to tackle the dispute between the two countries in a comprehensive manner. In 1998, given the domestic political situation in Ecuador, there was again a window of opportunity to reach agreement on the crucial issues.

The rhythm of the negotiations was carefully administered in order to allow trust to be built and permit different sectors of both societies to digest the necessary compromises. This is, of course, a conclusion reached post facto, therefore easily criticized for circular logic. Nevertheless, one could counterargue that each stage in the negotiation process did not take longer than a few months and that negotiators were able to produce some sense and measure of accomplishment at each stage, such as the establishment of the peace operation and the demilitarized zone, the outlining of the framework of negotiations, and the accomplishments of the commissions on confidence building and border integration before May 1998. On the other hand, although schedules were produced, deadlines were not treated as a critical issue, and the mediators managed to sustain the process in spite of the political instability in Ecuador and tension during the negotiations themselves.

Mediation is a form of international conflict management wherein high control over the process contrasts with low control over the outcome. The relation between the process of mediation and the context of a dispute largely explains the success or failure of the endeavor. In this case, the mediators were highly sensitive to the nature of the conflict, and their actions reflected the context of the conflict.

The need to rebuild the relation between the two countries both in subjective and objective terms was considered, given the possibilities offered by the regional and domestic environments and the deeply rooted sources of the conflict. The idea that relations between the two countries should be redrawn, or in the conceptual terms we have chosen to employ, that the enduring rivalry should end, was one of the pillars of the mediation process. The territorial dispute that marked this rivalry had to be tackled in both its objective and subjective dimensions. But, more importantly, the hostility between the parties had to be overcome. The attitudes of both parties had to change: each had to cease perceiving the other as a threat. Although more often framed in terms of the shift from a competitive (win-lose) situation to a cooperative (problem-solving) perspective in line with a rational choice paradigm, such a change in attitude has been shown to be a crucial variable in determining the outcome of international negotiations. The findings of previous research, in this respect, are borne out by the Peru-Ecuador case.[89]

The changes in the domestic environment reviewed earlier, particularly the linkage between peace and development, provided the conditions for new perspectives to gain ground. In fact, they can be discerned in proposals presented when Fujimori visited Ecuador in January 1992. As David Mares notes,

> President Alberto Fujimori's diplomatic openings to Ecuador in the early 1990s hinted of Peruvian willingness to put together a package deal linking economic development projects with some type of customs courtesies in Peruvian Amazonian ports in exchange for Ecuadorian recognition of a border demarcation that precludes sovereign access to the Marañon/Amazon rivers.[90]

The decision to adopt the principle of single undertaking allowed for a global agreement to be reached based on a balance between compromises made by both sides and the perception of mutual gains in the economic, political, military, and other realms. This can be observed in the last year of the process when the negotiations within the four commissions were clearly related. Thus, while the groups dealing with border integration and confidence-building measures reached agreements earlier, a fact that highlighted the possibilities of mutual gains, changes in the positions adopted by Ecuador in the demarcation commission and by Peru in the commerce and navigation commission opened the way to a final agreement.

The mediation process was structured on the premise that the involvement of the two contending parties was to be as active as possible. Although the guarantors were willing to invest diplomatic resources in the process, they continuously stressed that the responsibility for reaching political compromises and changing perspectives on bilateral relations lay with the disputants. Moreover, they constantly threatened to withdraw from the negotiations if the parties did not show willingness to move forward.[91] The guarantors were to make decisions only when both parties agreed in a consensual manner to this request. This position was expressed at the beginning of substantial negotiations when the parties met in Lima in January 1996.[92]

The risk taken by the guarantors when they decided to include Peruvian and Ecuadorian officers in the peace operation can be understood in this context. The responsibility for redefining relations on the ground was progressively transferred to the military establishments of the parties, further engaging them in the peace process.

The involvement of civil society in the negotiation process was considered fundamental by the mediators. The embassies of the four guarantor countries in both Peru and Ecuador sought to engage different sectors of these societies. As Ambassador Osmar Schofi mentions, the wider discussion of the issue in the press, at universities, and in parliament led Ecuadorians to conclude that it was necessary to overcome the dispute: when the proposition of a final arbitration was put to parliament, the prospect of approving it was thus enhanced.[93] The connection between official negotiations and societal contact can be observed most clearly in the work developed by the border integration commission, where representatives of the private sector were actively involved.

The participation of civil society in discussions on the conflict has already been discussed, but at this point the initiative of the Center for International Development and Conflict Management of the University of Maryland should be remembered. Although the initiative was not directly connected to the mediation process itself, this contact among ten Ecuadorians and ten Peruvians, representing diverse sectors of their societies, favored a new understanding of bilateral relations and focused attention on cooperative prospects for these relations. In fact, many of the participants in the Maryland group became members of the negotiating commissions created to deal with the four different areas of contention.[94]

A concern with cooperative security can also be discerned. The paradigmatic shift in the regional security context, outlined earlier, favored a focus on confidence-building measures. At the Regional Conference on Confidence-Building Measures and Security, held in Santiago only nine months after the end of the military confrontations, the deputy foreign ministers of Ecuador and Peru issued a joint declaration stressing their desire to normalize relations and outlining the confidence-building measures planned. The parties thereby expressed their support for the work developed by the Hemispheric Security Commission of the OAS.[95] In fact, as early as the second phase of the negotiations, a working group was created, responsible for generating confidence (Quito meeting, February 1996). The measures developed in the context of the observation mission and the accord signed at the end of the work of the commission on confidence building also indicate the relevance given by all parties to this aspect of the redefinition of relations.

NOTES

1. Ecuador acquired four Israeli Kfir fighters from Israel, and Peru bought sixteen Mig-29 fighters from Belarus. The acquisition of the Israeli jets by Ecuador generated concern, particularly since the United States gave authorization, as required by Israeli legislation.

2. "Communiqué of the Guarantor Countries of the Rio de Janeiro Protocol of 1942 to Ecuador and Peru," Brasília, January 27, 1995. Efraín F. Schereber, "La Declaración de Paz de Itamaraty," in Sandra Namihas, ed., *El Processo de Conversaciones para la Solución del Diferendo Peruano-Ecuatoriano* (Lima: Fondo Editorial de la Pontificia Universidad Católica del Perú, 2000), p. 55.

3. Permanent Council Resolution 642 (1015/95), OAS Official Document, January 30, 1995.

4. Marcel Biato notes that the efforts to bring the issue to the OAS and even to the United Nations Security Council were not supported by the

Brazilian government. Officials stressed that the mechanism available in this particular case was the protocol and discouraged other initiatives. Marcel Biato, "O Processo de Paz Peru-Equador," *Parcerias Estratégicas* 6 (1999), p. 62.

5. Marcelo F. de Córdoba, *Itamaraty Seiscientos Veintisiete Dias por la Paz* (Quito: V & O Gráficas, 1998), p. 85.

6. Bertha García Galegos, "New Perspectives on Using Diplomacy of the Resolution of the Ecuador-Peru Conflict," in Gabriel Marcella and Richard Downes, eds., *Security Cooperation in the Western Hemisphere: Resolving the Ecuador-Peru Conflict* (Miami: North-South Center Press, 1999), p. 200.

7. Ibid., pp. 197–198.

8. In September 1995, there was an attempt to reinterpret the meaning of the term *subsistent impasses* by the Peruvian side, narrowing it down to issues related to the Cenepa conflict and the definition of the demilitarized zone. See Biato, *O Processo de Paz,* p. 80.

9. David Scott Palmer, "The Search for Conflict Resolution: The Guarantors and the Peace Process in the Ecuador-Peru Dispute," in Marcella and Downes, eds., *Security Cooperation,* p. 29.

10. Francisco Tudela Van Breugel-Douglas, "Una Estrategia para La Paz," in Namihas, ed., *El Processo,* p. 81.

11. For a view of the Ecuadorian position see Adrián Bonilla, "The Ecuador-Peru Dispute: The Limits and Prospects for Negotiation and Conflict," in Marcella and Downes, eds., *Security Cooperation,* p. 77.

12. "Itamaraty Peace Declaration Between Peru and Ecuador," February 17, 1995, in Namihas, ed., *El Processo,* pp. 58–61.

13. Antonio Carlos do Nascimento, *Peru-Equador: Futuro de Paz/Perspectiva de Conflito* (Brasilia: Foreign Relations Ministry, Rio Branco Institute, 1997), p. 100.

14. On the substance of the meeting, see Biato, *O Processo de Paz,* pp. 82–84.

15. The group met five times between April 1996 and August 1997. Raúl Patino Alvistur, "Acuerdo de Constituición de la Comisión Binacoinal Sobre Medidas de Confianza Mutua y de Seguridad," in Namihas, ed., *El Processo,* p. 528.

16. "Santiago Accord," October 29, 1996, in Marcel Biato, *O Processo de Paz Equador-Peru e a Solução Pacífica de Controvérsias* (Brasilia: Instituto Rio Branco–LVI Curso de Altos Estudos, 2001).

17. The negotiations would take place according to the framework established by the following documents: the 1942 Rio de Janeiro Protocol, the Itamaraty Declaration (February 17, 1995), the Buenos Aires Communiqué (June 19, 1995), the Quito Accord (February 23, 1996), and the Santiago Accord (October 29, 1996).

18. "Santiago Accord," October 29, 1996, paragraph four.

19. "Protocol of Peace, Friendship and Borders Between Peru and Ecuador," February 14, 1942, in Marcella and Downes, eds., *Security Cooperation,* p. 239.

20. Palmer, "The Search for Conflict Resolution," p. 28.

21. The foreign minister of Peru was one of the hostages in the embassy, and President Bucaran postponed a visit to Lima. Abdala Bucaran was officially ousted from office due to allegations of mental incapacity.

22. For a description of these talks, see Biato, *O Processo de Paz,* pp. 94–95.

23. "Reflections for Conversations Between Ecuador and Peru to Take Place in Brasília, November 1997," November 19, 1997, in Biato, *O Processo de Paz,* pp. 252–253. Basic ideas present in the proposals presented by Alberto Fujimori in 1991 can be found in this document.

24. For a description of these talks see Biato, *O Processo de Paz,* pp. 102–103.

25. Drago Kisic Wagner, "Acuerdo Amplio de Integración Fronteriza, Desarrollo y Vecindad: Estrategia y Negociación," in Namihas, ed., *El Processo,* p. 430.

26. Raúl Patino Alvistur, "Acurdo de Constituición de la Comisión Binacoinal Sobre Medidas de Confianza Mutua y de Seguridad," in Namihas, ed., *El Processo,* p. 534.

27. Jorge Lázaro Geldres, "El Alcance de la Comisión Binacional Peruano-Ecuatoriana Sobre Medidas de Fomento," in Namihas, ed., *El Processo.* First-generation confidence-building measures stem from the 1975 Helsinki Conference. Second-generation confidence-building measures were discussed in the context of the Stockholm Conference, which took place between 1984 and 1986. In this case, apart from greater availability of information on maneuvers, the measures included regulation of verification. Enrique Obando, "Perú y los Procesos de Verificación," in Francisco Rojas Aravena, ed., *Medidas de Confianza Mutua: Verificación* (Santiago: FLACSO, 1996).

28. Brazilian Foreign Office, Information n. 393, October 23, 1998, p. 17.

29. Article 6 calls for Ecuador to have access to the same benefits as Brazil and Colombia in the area. A treaty regarding free navigation was signed between Brazil and Peru in 1909 and between Peru and Colombia in 1922 and 1934. Alfonso de Los Heros Perez-Albela, "Tratado de Comercio y Navegación: Estrategia y Negociación," in Namihas, ed., *El Processo,* p. 314.

30. For a description of these debates see Biato, *O Processo de Paz,* pp. 112–113.

31. Brazilian Foreign Office, Information n. 393, October 23, 1998, p. 16.

32. Ibid., pp. 18–19.

33. The accords were presented in Lima on June 3, 1998, at a forum organized by CEPEI (Peruvian Center for International Studies—University of the Pacific) and in Quito at an event organized by CORDES on June 11, 1998. Wagner, "Acuerdo Amplio," in Namihas, ed., *El Processo,* p. 441.

34. Biato, *O Processo de Paz,* p. 125.

35. D. S. Palmer, "Missed Opportunities and Misplaced Nationalism,"

in Tommie Sue Montgomery, ed., *Peacemaking and Democratization in the Western Hemisphere* (Miami: North-South Center, 2000), pp. 247–278.

36. Gabriel Marcella and Richard Downes, "The Ecuador-Peru Dispute and Conflict Resolution in the Americas," in Marcella and Downes, eds., *Security Cooperation,* p. 232.

37. Biato, *O Processo de Paz,* p. 136.

38. The result of the vote was Ecuador, 96 for, 21 against; Peru, 86 for, 26 against.

39. "The Guarantor Presidents' Letter," October 23, 1998, in Marcella and Downes, eds., *Security Cooperation,* p. 246.

40. Perez-Albela, "Tratado de Comercio y Navegación," in Namihas, ed., *El Processo,* pp. 323–324.

41. Brazilian Foreign Office, Information n. 393, October 23, 1998, pp. 9–15.

42. When peace missions were set up in the hemisphere, they were generated at the United Nations. These included the United Nations Observer Group in Central America (ONUCA), the Observer Mission to El Salvador (ONUSAL), the United Nations Mission in Haiti (UNMIH), and the United Nations Verification Mission to Guatemala (MINIGUA).

43. The documents that regulate the creation and functioning of the mission are the Peace Declaration of Itamaraty of February 1995; the Definition of Procedures for MOMEP, March 10, 1995; the Definition of Procedures for MOMEP, August 11, 1995; the Rules of MOMEP, May 1, 1996 (reviewed on October 20, 1997, and March 30, 1999); and the minutes of the meetings of the MOMEP Committee.

44. See Glenn Weidner, "Peacekeeping in the Upper Cenepa Valley: A Regional Response to Crisis," in Marcella and Downes, eds., *Security Cooperation.* General Claudio Barbosa de Fiqueiredo, "MOMEP: Una Mision Cumplida," *Revista de Fuerzas Armadas del Ecuador. Verde-Oliva,* Special Edition (Brasília: Brazilian Army, 1999), n. 166.

45. "Montevideo Declaration," February 28, 1995, in Biato, *O Processo de Paz.*

46. Weidner, "Peacekeeping," in Marcella and Downes, eds., *Security Cooperation,* p. 61.

47. Ronald L. Jepperson, Alexander Wendt, and Peter J. Katzenstein, "Norms, Identity, and Culture in National Security," in Peter Katzenstein, ed., *The Culture of National Security* (New York: Columbia University Press, 1996).

48. The First International Conference of American States took place in Washington during six months in 1889–1890. There were formed the International Union of American States (whose name changed to Union of American Republics in 1910 and then to Union of American States in 1928) and the Commercial Bureau of American Republics (replaced in 1910 by the Pan American Union as the secretariat for the inter-American system). Several International Conferences of American States have since taken place.

49. See G. Pope Atkins, *Latin America in the International Political*

System (Boulder: Westview Press, 1995), and Gerson Moura, "A Segurança Coletiva Continental: O Sistema Interamericano, O TIAR e a Guerra Fria," in José Guilhon de Alburquerque, ed., *Sessenta Años de Política Externa Brasileira* (São Paulo: Cultura Editores Associados, 1996).

50. Since the end of the nineteenth century, the American states had been discussing and signing treaties and conventions related to the peaceful settlement of disputes. At the 1945 conference, leaders perceived the importance of coordinating the various measures and finally signed the Pact of Bogotá in 1948.

51. The Inter-American Conference was the general decisionmaking body of the organization, but major business was conducted by the foreign ministers' meeting after the Caracas Conference of 1954. The 1967 Protocol of Buenos Aires abolished the Inter-American Conference and created the General Assembly as the new supreme organ of the OAS.

52. Carlos Calvo, an Argentine jurist, challenged the European position that foreign residents should have special rights with regard to pecuniary claims, stressing that intervention by foreign governments to enforce the claims of their own citizens was illegal. Luis Drago, Argentine foreign minister, defended the illegality of armed intervention referring to public debt, in the context of the Venezuelan debt crisis at the beginning of the twentieth century.

53. Mares discusses this pattern of behavior, stressing the bilateral approach chosen in most cases. David Mares and Steven A. Bernstein, "The Use of Force in Latin American Interstate Relations," in Jorge I. Dominguez, ed., *International Security & Democracy: Latin America and the Caribbean in the Post–Cold War Era* (Pittsburgh: University of Pittsburgh Press, 1998), p. 42.

54. At the Twentieth Meeting of Consultation of Ministers of Foreign Affairs, convened in April 1982, the representatives decided not to invoke sanctions, as Argentina had requested, although they did support Argentine claims to sovereignty. In addition, the United States ended its neutrality on April 30, supporting the United Kingdom.

55. The Contadora Group (Colombia, Mexico, Panama, and Venezuela) first met in January 1983 and in July 1985, the Contadora Support Group was created (Argentina, Brazil, Peru, and Uruguay). The Rio Group was created in December 1986, when the members of the Contadora Group and Contadora Support Group agreed to generate a Permanent Mechanism for Consultation and Political Coordination. The aim was to prevent unilateral intervention by the United States in view of the growing instability in Central America. In 1990, Chile and Ecuador joined the group. See Francisco R. Aravena, "The Rio Group and Regional Security in Latin America," in Olga Pellicer, *Regional Mechanisms and International Security in Latin America* (Tokyo: United Nations University Press, 1998).

56. Augusto Varas, "Cooperative Hemispheric Security After the Cold War," in Pellicer, *Regional Mechanisms*, p. 29.

57. Argentina and Chile had, in 1984, signed a treaty resolving the dispute over the islands of Picton, Lennox, and Nueva in the Beagle Channel.

58. President Oscar Arias of Costa Rica proposed a peace plan on the basis of which the Esquipulas II Accords were signed on August 17, 1987. A permanent cease-fire was reached in Nicaragua in April 1990 and in El Salvador in February 1992.

59. See Jorge I. Dominguez, "Security, Peace, and Democracy in Latin America and the Caribbean Challenges for the Post–Cold War Era," in Jorge I. Dominguez, ed., *International Security & Democracy.*

60. In March 1994, the Special Committee on the Charter of the United Nations and on the Strengthening of the Role of the Organization approved a Declaration on the Enhancement of Cooperation Between the United Nations and Regional Arrangements or Agencies in the Maintenance of International Peace and Security, United Nations Document A/AC.182/ 1994/CRP.3/add.3. The OAS and the UN worked together in the cases of both Haiti and Nicaragua. On cooperation between the OAS and the UN, see Margarida Diéguez, "Regional Mechanisms for the Maintenance of Peace and Security in the Western Hemisphere," in Pellicer, ed., *Regional Mechanisms.*

61. For the concept of cooperative security, see Ashton B. Carter, William J. Perry, and John D. Stenbruner, *A New Concept of Cooperative Security* (Washington, D.C.: Brookings Institution, 1992) and Janee E. Nolan, ed., *Global Engagement: Cooperation and Security in the 21st Century* (Washington, D.C.: Brookings Institution, 1994). Hernán Patiño Meyer, Argentina's ambassador to the OAS from 1992 to 1995, focused on the concept and related issues. See Permanent Council of the Organization of American States, Special Committee on Hemisphere Security, Support for a New Concept of Hemisphere Security: Co-operative Security, OEA/Ser.G,GE/SH-12/93 rev. 1, May 17, 1993. For a discussion of the role played by the concept in the Latin American context, see Jorge Domínguez, "Security, Peace, and Democracy," in Jorge Domínguez, ed., *International Security & Democracy*; Patrice Franko, "Patterns of Military Procurement in Latin America: Implications for U.S. Regional Policy," in Marcella and Downes, eds., *Security Cooperation;* Ivelaw Griffith, "Security Collabora- tion and Confidence-Building in the Americas," in Domínguez, ed., *International Security & Democracy.*

62. The bilateral and multilateral contacts between military institutions have increased, and the Annual Conference of the Chiefs of the Army, Navy, and Air Forces has been institutionalized. See Francisco Rojas Aravena, "Confidence Building Measures and Strategic Balance: A Step Toward Expansion and Stability," in Joseph S. Tulchin and Francisco Rojas Aravena, eds., *Strategic Balance and Confidence Building Measures* (Stanford: Stanford University Press, 1998).

63. See Paul Buchanam, "Chameleon, Tortoise, or Toad: The Changing U.S. Security Role in Contemporary Latin America," in Dominguez, ed., *International Security & Democracy*; John Cope, "United States View of Strategic Balance in the Americas," in Tulchin and Aravena, eds., *Strategic Balance.*

64. Celso Lafer and Gelson Fonseca Jr., "Questões para a Diplomacia

No Contexto Internacional das Polaridades Indefinidas," in Gélson Fonseca Jr. and Sérgio Henrique Nabuco de Castro, eds., *Temas de Política Externa Brasileira*.

65. We refer to the widening and internationalization of the concept of security. See Monica Herz, "Brazilian Perspectives on the Redefinition of the Concept of Security," ACUNS 12th Annual Meeting, New York, 1999.

66. Jeanne Hey, "Ecuadoran Foreign Policy Since 1979: Ideological Cycles or a Trend Towards Neoliberalism?" *Journal of Interamerican Studies and World Affairs* 37, 4 (1995).

67. For more details on the Borja initiative, see Chapter 3.

68. Bruce Kay,"'Fujipopulism' and the Liberal State in Peru, 1990–1995," *Journal of Interamerican Studies and World Affairs* 38, 4 (1996).

69. Peter Flindell Klarén, *Peru: Society and Nationhood in the Andes* (New York: Oxford University Press, 2000).

70. Mahuad was himself deposed by a military coup in January 2000, in the context of serious social unrest created by his economic policies and by charges of corruption.

71. Diego Cordovez, *Nuestra Propuesta Inconclusa. Ecuador-Perú: Del Inmovilismo al Acuerdo de Brasilia* (Quito: Corporación Editora Nacional).

72. Former chancellor Diego Cordovez coincides in the evaluation that, once the framework was accepted, the outcome of the negotiations was necessarily compromised against Ecuador's claim to sovereign access to the Marañon and Amazon Rivers.

73. Diego Cordovez, *Nuestra Propuesta Inconclusa.*

74. Interview with Ambassador Eduardo Ponce, April 4, 2001.

75. For example, the Corporación de Estudios Sociales (CORDES) held a seminar in December 1992, and the Centro Peruano de Estudios Internacionales (CEPEI) held a seminar in October 1993. Bertha García Gallegos, "New Perspectives," in Marcella and Downes, eds., *Security Cooperation.*

76. For commentary on the relationship between Fujimori's handling of the process and the Peruvian press, see Carlos Reyna Izaguirre, "Diplomacia Presidencial y Mediatización de la Política," in Adrián Bonilla, ed., *Ecuador-Perú: Horizontes de la Negociación y el Conflicto* (Quito: FLACSO, 1999).

77. Interview with Dr. Francisco Tudela, Lima, April 3, 2001.

78. Malcom N. Shaw, *International Law* (Cambridge: Cambridge University Press, 2000), chapter 18.

79. Jacob Bercovitch, "The Structure and Diversity of Mediation in International Relations," in Bercovitch and Rubin, eds., *Mediation in International Relations: Multiple Approaches to Conflict Management* (London: Macmillan, 1992).

80. The rules dealing with conciliation were elaborated in the 1928 General Act on the Pacific Settlement of International Disputes (revised in 1949). The heyday of conciliation commissions was the interwar period.

81. The United Nations Sixth Committee approved a report on a code

of rule on conciliation in 1996, in the context of a renewed interest in the subject. J. G. Merrills, *International Dispute Settlement* (Cambridge: Cambridge University Press, 1998), p. 79.

82. Francisco Rezek, *Direito dos Tratados* (Rio de Janeiro: Editorial Forense, 1984).

83. In the case of the guarantors of the Swiss Confederation in 1815 and of the guarantors of the Treaty of Locarno in 1925, the responsibility regarded the defense of the borders. Van Breugel-Douglas, "Una Estrategia," in Namihas, ed., *El Proceso*, p. 69.

84. Merrills, *International Dispute*, p. 34.

85. J. Bercovitch, "The Structure and Diversity," in Bercovitch and Rubin, *Mediation in International Relations*, p. 9.

86. As Lawrence Susskind and Eileen Babbitt note, strong leadership is one of the preconditions for effective mediation. Lawrence Susskind and Eileen Babbitt, "Overcoming the Obstacles to Effective Mediation of International Disputes," in S. Touval and I. W. Zartman, eds., *International Mediation in Theory and Practice* (Boulder: Westview, 1985), p. 33.

87. S. Touval and I. W. Zartman, "Introduction: Mediation in Theory," in Touval and Zartman, eds., *International Mediation*.

88. On this issue see interview with Fabian Novak, Lima, April 2, 2001.

89. Daniel Druckman, "Negotiating in the International Context," in I. W. Zartman and J. L. Rasmussen, eds., *Peacemaking in International Conflict: Methods and Techniques* (Washington, D.C.: U.S. Institute of Peace, 1999).

90. Mares, "Political-Military Coordination," in Marcella and Downes, eds., *Security Cooperation*, p. 173.

91. Interview with Ambassador Ivan Canabrava, Brasilia, April 4, 2001.

92. Biato, *O Processo de Paz*, p. 82.

93. Interview with Ambassador Osmar Schofi, Brasilia, April 4, 2001.

94. Maryland Group, *Ecuador-Perú: Hacia una Iniciativa Democrática y Cooperativa de Resolución de Conflitos* (College Park: Maryland Group, 1998). Bertha Garcia Gallegos, Edy Kaufman, Oscar Schiappa-Pietra, and Saúl Sosnowski, *Ecuador y Perú: Estrategias para la Resolución del Conflicto* (College Park: Maryland Group, 1998).

95. Jorge Lázaro Geldres, "El Alcance de la Comisión Binacional Peruano-Ecuatoriana Sobre Medidas de Fomento," in Namihas, ed., *El Processo*, p. 550.

5

Conclusion

Our research has explored the mediation process that resulted in the signing of an agreement between two countries that had been involved in a conflict that shaped their bilateral relations and their identities as participants in the regional and international systems. The negotiation process that engaged Peru, Ecuador, and the four mediators was conducted from the perspective of redefining the bilateral relation in a comprehensive manner. This was only possible because four relevant actors chose to focus on the negotiation process and allocate important resources for this purpose. On the other hand, the regional and domestic environments offered the necessary objective and subjective conditions for the undertaking of negotiations that led to the final resolution of the conflict. This experience is valuable for the understanding and pursuit of international negotiations in three different settings: the mediation of international conflict in general, the mediation of enduring rivalries specifically, and conflict resolution in Latin America in particular.

In cases of protracted disputes, such as this one, it is very difficult to determine the moment in time when rivalry reaches its termination. Most scholars identify the end of a rivalry according to a period of time, such as ten years, in which additional militarized disputes do not occur.[1] However, in the context of rivalries, peace is defined in terms of the redefinition of attitudes, when militarized means are no longer considered a policy option. Thus the end of a war or the resolution of one or a set of contentious issues does not necessarily signal the end of rivalry. One criterion, adopted by Scott Bennett, focuses on the settlement of the issue or issues that define the rivalry.[2] The connection between enduring rivalries and territorial disputes has been stressed at several points in earlier chapters. Although this is not a sufficient indicator, the settlement of issues may play an important role in changing attitudes regarding the "other," a key aspect of the definition of rivalry we have adopted.

According to the standard applied by the literature on rivalries, not enough time has passed to allow us to establish that the rivalry between Peru and Ecuador has been terminated, although three years have passed since the signing of the Brasilia Accords, and seven years have passed since the Cenepa War. Still, the agreements reached effectively settled their territorial dispute and the border has been finally demarcated.

Neither the signing of an agreement nor the passing of time seems sufficient to guarantee the end of a rivalry: only a permanent change in attitudes, the crucial actor dimension, will do this. Agents can only redefine their relationship with their foe once their identities cease to be determined by the rivalry, and such a shift is only possible when the other is no longer perceived as a threat. In this case the interactive process itself, which reconstructed the relationship, is the clearest indication that attitudes have undergone change. Indeed, as we have noticed, a disposition toward change was present even before the Cenepa War, and the mediators were able to structure the negotiation process with this end in view. The redefinition of interests and identities, as outlined above, occurs not only at the interaction level but also at the unit and systemic levels. The domestic and regional environments allowed for a change in interests and values in both Peru and Ecuador.

Several strategies employed in the mediation process spurred the redefinition of bilateral relations, such as the adoption of the principle of single undertaking, the commitment and involvement demanded from both Peru and Ecuador, the engagement of both societies, the focus on the potentialities of interdependence, and respect for the subjective requirements of each party. The compromise reached accommodated basic elements of national identities, while also allowing for change. Thus Ecuador acquired an outlet to the Amazon Basin, and Peru attained a final and definite definition of its border. These strategies favored the ending of rivalry in a context of "intimacy," where the identities of the two countries were at stake. The process allowed for an evolving interaction among the negotiators, over almost four years, to promote changes in interests and identities on a larger scale. Hence the path undertaken did not focus solely on defusing tensions or on the postponement of difficult negotiations. Rather, the mediation process diminished the cost of difficult decisions on the part of both governments, and the mediators shared in the cost and investment of negotiations. The involvement of the guarantor countries in a more active manner than envisaged by the 1942 Rio Protocol sustained the process and granted it more creative and flexible features.

The domestic and regional conditions of the mid-1990s, which permitted this process to evolve, should be borne in mind. Among these figured the development of an acute sensibility among relevant social and political actors and policymakers in both Peru and Ecuador to the imperatives of a global order that imposed heavy costs on countries involved in armed conflicts that threatened regional stability and negatively affected the investment environment. Peru and Ecuador were involved in processes of redefinition of interests and identities that reduced the relevance of the territorial issue vis-à-vis the goal of integration in the global political economy.

The norm of conflict resolution by peaceful means and the idea that peace is a regional asset, which became a prevailing value in the 1990s, favored the active involvement of the guarantors and the perception that a final solution to the dispute should be found. These values and the norm of peaceful resolution of conflicts shaped both the posture of the guarantors and the changing identities of the disputants.

The norm of nonintervention and the legalist tradition cherished by the Latin American decisionmaking elite were preserved. The time frame chosen by negotiators allowed for the accommodation of domestic concerns and the building of trust and confidence among the parties. Thus, although the guarantors did at the final stage perform as arbitrators, they did so only after requests by the parties were filed and this specific jurisdiction was approved by both legislatures. Moreover, the mission deployed in the area of the conflict also performed solely as a peacekeeping mission. As the first peace operation in South America in the post–Cold War era, it did not inaugurate more interventionist operations in the area. A tendency to act in the context of ad hoc multilateral arrangements is reasserted by this experience. The use of informal mechanisms may also be seen as a policy of sovereignty preservation. In this particular case, the use of an ad hoc multilateral arrangement guaranteed a basic framework for the initiation of negotiations. Nevertheless, the success of the mediation process may confirm a tendency already in place.

The structure of the negotiations and the final agreements also express a move toward cooperative security, the players involved having sought to create an environment of trust and confidence at all levels. The manner in which the conflict evolved in 1995 and on other occasions can be understood in terms of the lack of effective confidence-building measures among the parties. This perspective is reflected in the Act of Brasilia, where confidence-building measures are cited as a long-term objective.

An analysis of the behavior of the two countries in the aftermath of the agreements indicates that the rivalry has ended.[3] The implementation of the accords, regardless of delays generated by the lack of funds, the changes in official positions, and the greater coordination of the foreign policies of the two countries in international forums, not to mention the growing cooperation in areas such as drug and arms traffic, confirms the magnitude of the changes. Visits by the president of Ecuador to Peru in August 1999 and by the president of Peru to Ecuador in October 1999 set the scene for the new terms of the countries' peacetime relations, a neighborhood commission having been created and several accords having been signed. More than thirty bilateral accords, in several areas, have been negotiated and subscribed to in line with the Integration, Development and Neighborhood Accord; the commerce and navigation centers of Pijuayal and Saramiriza have been planed;[4] and the volume of global trade between the countries reached U.S.$411 million in 2000, a 59 percent increase relative to 1998 levels.[5]

POLICY RECOMMENDATIONS

The negotiation process analyzed in this research allows us to reach a number of conclusions regarding peaceful conflict resolution and the role of international mediation: some policy recommendations follow. The intervention of international negotiators may be a necessary mechanism even when domestic and systemic conditions are favorable. Mediation, specifically, is a conflict management mechanism where the availability of concrete nonbinding proposals may be extremely useful. Moreover, the sharing of costs, in the context of the internationalization of negotiations, is a central advantage of this mechanism.

Mediators should take an active part in administering the negotiation process, taking into account the sensibilities and limits of the contending parts, but at the same time making active suggestions. Apart from setting the framework, the mediators should attend in particular to the rhythm of the negotiations, allowing for a proper balance between the necessary time for each society to digest the compromises on the table and the constitution of a sense of accomplishment after each stage.

When conditions allow, the mediation process should be geared toward conflict resolution, not solely conflict management, even if the time frame must be expanded. The role played by concrete and imaginative proposals that set a context for the negotiations and the use of a wide array of strategies should be stressed. The principle of single undertaking was shown in this research to be a particularly useful tactic, allowing for a wide view of the compromises made by all parts and the perspective of mutual gains to be displayed before agreements were signed. The interconnectedness between conflict management and conflict resolution is highlighted by an analysis of the Peru-Ecuador negotiations. The insulation of the military confrontation from the political negotiations may be fundamental for the successful outcome of the process.

Although this research does not corroborate the argument that democracies tend to solve disputes peacefully, it does indicate that growing interdependence both in bilateral and global terms favors the peaceful resolution of conflicts. The generation of interest groups oriented toward interdependence and the involvement of society at large in the modification of the basic features of the relationship through the media and the educational system favor this development. Therefore the participation of civil society in discussions on the conflict is fundamental, and when possible, the creation of lines of communication between official negotiations and nonofficial contacts is useful.

Attempts to negotiate in the context of enduring rivalries must take into account subjective and objective aspects of the relationship, in particular the redefinition of identities and interests, the generation of incentives, and recognition of interdependence. In such cases, the mediation process should allow for a redefinition of the relationship and the change of attitudes. This can be achieved both through procedural propositions such as the time frame; the definition of the phases of the negotiations; and the involvement of different actors from the societies in conflict and through concrete proposals regarding borders, common use of resources, commerce, cultural and technological cooperation, and confidence-building measures. When a territorial dispute marks a rivalry, as is often the case, rivalry termination will only occur if this dispute is tackled. This redefinition should take place at the unit and systemic levels. The investment necessary to deal with such conflicts should only be made when a significant change indicates the possibility of success. Such changes can be "based" on the unit or systemic level or both: they may involve an important event, such as the outcome of the 1995 war; social, cultural and economic changes; changes in the balance of power; or shifts in the institutional environment. When a window of opportunity and the disposition to invest in a mediation process are available, enduring rivalries can be overcome.

Regarding conflict resolution in Latin America specifically, this research indicates a strong potential for the use of mediation as a valid mechanism in handling interstate conflict, the peaceful conflict resolution norm having strong roots in the region and regional powers having the will and resources to engage in such endeavors. The remaining border disputes in the region should be dealt with in a peaceful way, probably with the use of mediation and arbitration mechanisms. This recommendation requires review in the case of intrastate conflict, given the likewise deeply rooted norm of nonintervention and defense of state sovereignty. For these cases, the inter-American system has yet to generate reliable institutions based on clear universalistic principles and norms, although much has been achieved in the last decade.

Analysis of this case supports a view of the effectiveness of ad hoc mechanisms in Latin America. International organizations, such as the United Nations or the Organization of American States, should in certain circumstances be left as alternative forums for debate and for the definition of norms of conduct. In cases where an existing ad hoc mechanism favors continuity, it should not be dismantled or set aside. This research supports the view that specific norms and procedures geared toward a specific interaction, although they do not provide a complete answer to a dispute, should once established be used, redefined, and reconstructed, rather than abandoned. Furthermore, the convenience of the role of a specific coalition or group of actors with common objectives should be explored. Since the establishment of common objectives or a common agenda may be circumscribed in time and space, a low level of institutionalization may be appropriate. The flexibility provided by ad hoc mechanisms is an asset that may prove fundamental in international negotiations, allowing for the necessary changes in the negotiation environment and the addition of creative devices. In Latin America specifically, the OAS is viewed with skepticism given the high level of control exerted by the Unites States over this organization. In alternative settings, other regional actors may feel they have more room for maneuver and may commit greater resources.

Nevertheless this investigation does not indicate that ad hoc instruments are necessarily more efficient. On the contrary, the negotiations were successful partly because the mediation process was embedded in a culture of peaceful conflict resolution and boosted by the idea that the region should be "sold" as one characterized by peace and stability. This culture was partially constructed in the context of the OAS and previous regional organizations and supported by processes evolving within the United Nations System, particularly after the end of the Cold War. The negotiation framework had to be modified in order to allow for the guarantors to become active mediators in a new institutional and ideational environment.

The idea that conflict resolution processes in Latin America benefit from the loss of the political veto power of the military establishment is upheld by our findings, although the influence of the military elite in policy formulation and implementation regarding international conflict remains a significant factor. This is a sensitive issue in a region where the relation between the military and civil authorities is not always guided by the institutional bearings of liberal democracy. The insulation of military confrontations from diplomatic negotiations, the influence exerted by mediators on states, and the internationalization of negotiations may all encourage this tendency.

Finally, the proposition that conflict resolution mechanisms should be regionalized is supported by this research, the knowledge and interest of the international mediators having enhanced the effectiveness of the process.

NOTES

1. Goertz and Diehl, "Enduring Rivalries: Theoretical Constructs and Empirical Patterns," *International Studies Quarterly* 37 (1995).

2. D. Scott Bennet, "Measuring Rivalry Termination," *Journal of Conflict Resolution* 41, 2 (1997). The author writes from a rational choice perspective and thus is concerned with the change in the cost-benefit calculation of the actors. In this research this is considered a question that begs further inquiry.

3. A survey undertaken by Promperú shows significant changes in the opinions of both Peruvians and Ecuadorians between the ages of 18 and 30 in the first year after the signing of the agreements. See *Analisis Internacional,* no. 17 (Lima: CEPEI, 1999), pp. 251–263.

4. *El Ejercicio de la Paz,* Informe 2000 (Quito: Ministério de Relaciones Exteriores-Republica del Ecuador, 2000).

5. Data from the Ministry of Foreign Relation of Peru, available online at http://www.rree.gob.pe (April 15, 2001).

Bibliography

"Acuerdo Amplio Peruano-Ecuatoriano de Integración Fronteriza: Desarrollo y Vecindad," *Analisis Internacional,* no. 15 (Lima: CEPEI, 1998), pp. 333–341.

Aguas, Luis, lieutenant colonel and commander of the 26th Group of the Ecuadorian Army Special Forces. Interview with authors, Quito, April 5, 2001.

Alfonso de Los Heros, Perez-Albela, "Tratado de Comercio y Navegación: Estrategia y Negociación," in Sandra Namihas (ed.), *El Processo de Conversaciones para la Solución del Diferendo Peruano-Ecuatoriano* (Lima: Fondo Editorial de la Pontificia Universidad Católica del Perú, 2000).

Alvistur, Raúl Patino, "Acuerdo de Constituición de la Comisión Binacional Sobre Medidas de Confianza Mutua y de Seguridad," in Sandra Namihas (ed.), *El Processo de Conversaciones para la Solución del Diferendo Peruano-Ecuatoriano* (Lima: Fondo Editorial de la Pontificia Universidad Católica del Perú, 2000).

Anderson, Benedict, *Imagined Communities: Reflections on the Origin and Spread of Nationalism* (London: Verso, 1991).

Aravena, Francisco Rojas, "Confidence Building Measures and Strategic Balance: A Step Toward Expansion and Stability," in Joseph S. Tulchin and Francisco Rojas Aravenas (eds.), *Strategic Balance and Confidence Building Measures in the Americas* (Stanford, CA: Stanford University Press, 1998).

―――, "The Rio Group and Regional Security in Latin America," in Olga Pellicer (ed.), *Regional Mechanisms and International Security in Latin America* (Tokyo: United Nations University, 1998).

Atkins, G. Pope, *Latin America in the International Political System* (Boulder: Westview Press, 1995).

Bennet, D. Scott, "Measuring Rivalry Termination," *Journal of Conflict Resolution* 41, 2 (1997): 227–254.

Bercovitch, Jacob, "The Structure and Diversity of Mediation in International Relations," in Jacob Bercovitch and Jeffrey Z. Rubin (eds.), *Mediation in International Relations: Multiple Approaches to Conflict Management* (London: Macmillan, 1992).

Bercovitch, Jacob, Paul Diehl, and Gary Goertz, "The Management and Termination of Protracted Interstate Conflicts: Conceptual and Empirical Considerations," *Millennium: Journal of International Studies* 26, 3 (1997): 751–769.

Biato, Marcel, *O Processo de Paz Equador-Peru e a Solução Pacífica de Controvérsias* (Brasília: Instituto Rio Branco and LVI Curso de Altos Estudos, 2001).

———, "O Processo de Paz Peru-Equador," *Parcerias Estratégicas*, no. 6 (Março 1999): 241–247.

Bonilla, Adrian, "The Ecuador-Peru Dispute: The Limits and Prospects for Negotiation and Conflict," in G. Marcella and R. Downes (eds.), *Security Cooperation in the Western Hemisphere: Resolving the Ecuador-Peru Conflict* (Miami: North-South Center Press, 1999).

———, "Fuerza, Conflicto, y Negociacion: Proceso Politico de la Relacion Entre Ecuador y Peru," in Adrián Bonilla (ed.), *Ecuador-Peru: Horizontes de la Negociacion y el Conflicto* (Quito: FLACSO, Ecuador, 1999).

———, "Proceso Politico e Intereses Nacionales en el Conflicto Peru-Ecuador," *Nueva Sociedad* 143 (1996): 30–40.

——— (ed.), *Ecuador-Peru: Horizontes de la Negociación y el Conflicto* (Quito: FLACSO Ecuador, 1999).

Brazilian Foreign Office, Information n. 393 and n. 382. October 23, 1998.

Buchanam, Paul, "Chameleon, Tortoise, or Toad: The Changing U.S. Security Role in Contemporary Latin America," in Jorge I. Dominguez (ed.), *International Security & Democracy: Latin America and the Caribbean in the Post–Cold War Era* (Pittsburgh: University of Pittsburgh Press, 1998).

Burga, M., "La Imagen Nacional del Perú en Su Historia," in A. Bonilla (ed.), *Ecuador-Perú: Horizontes de la Negociación y el Conflicto* (Quito: FLACSO, 1999).

Bustamante, Fernando, "The Question of Confidence Building Measures in the Andean Subregion," in Joseph S. Tulchin and Francisco Rojas Aravenas (eds.), *Strategic Balance and Confidence Building Measures in the Americas* (Stanford, CA: Stanford University Press, 1998).

Calvert, P., *Boundary Disputes in Latin America* (London: Institute for the Study of Conflict, 1983).

Canabrava, Ivan, chief Brazilian negotiator. Interview with the authors, Brasilia, April 4, 2001.

Carter, Ashton B., William J. Perry, and John D. Stenbruner, *A New Concept of Cooperative Security* (Washington, D.C.: Brookings Institution, 1992).

"Communiqué of the Guarantor Countries of the Rio de Janeiro Protocol of 1942 to Ecuador and Peru," Brasília, January 27, 1995, in Marcel Biato, *O Processo de Paz Equador-Peru e a Solução Pacífica de Controvérsias* (Brasília: Instituto Rio Branco and LVI Curso de Altos Estudos, 2001).

Conaghan, Catherine M., "Loose Parties, 'Floating' Politicians, and Institutional Stress: Presidentialism in Ecuador, 1979–1988," in J. J. Linz and A. Valenzuela (eds.), *The Failure of Presidential Democracy: The Case of Latin America* (Baltimore: Johns Hopkins University Press, 1994).

Cope, John A., "United States View of Strategic Balance in the Americas," in Joseph S. Tulchin and Francisco Rojas Aravenas (eds.), *Strategic Balance and Confidence Building Measures in the Americas* (Stanford, CA: Stanford University Press, 1998).

Cordoba, Marcelo Fernandez de, *Itamaraty Seiscientos: Veintisiete Dias por la Paz* (Quito: V&O Gráficas, 1998).

Cordovez, Diego, *Nuestra Propuesta Inconclusa. Ecuador-Perú: Del Inmovilismo al Acuerdo de Brasilia* (Quito: Corporación Editora Nacional, 2000).

Corrêa, Luiz Felipe de Seixas, "Introdução," in Fundação Alexandre Gusmão (ed.), *A Palavra do Brasil nas Nações Unidas* (Brasília: FUNAG, 2000).

Costa, Thomaz Guedes, "Strategic Balance, Brazil, and Western Hemispheric Security," in Joseph S. Tulchin and Francisco Rojas Aravenas (eds.), *Strategic Balance and Confidence Building Measures in the Americas* (Stanford, CA: Stanford University Press, 1998).

"Declaration of the Guarantor Countries of the Rio de Janeiro 1942 Protocol," February 6, 1995. *Resenha de Política Exterior do Brasil,* no. 76 (1995): 297–299.

Diéguez, Margarida, "Regional Mechanisms for the Maintenance of Peace and Security in the Western Hemisphere," in Olga Pellicer (ed.), *Regional Mechanisms and International Security in Latin America* (Tokyo: United Nations University, 1998).

Dominguez, Jorge, "Security, Peace, and Democracy in Latin America and the Caribbean: Challenges for the Post–Cold War Era," in Jorge I. Dominguez (ed.), *International Security & Democracy: Latin America and the Caribbean in the Post–Cold War Era* (Pittsburgh: University of Pittsburgh Press, 1998).

Druckman, Danniel, "Negotiating in the International Context," in I. W. Zartman and J. L. Rasmussen (eds.), *Peacemaking in International Conflict Methods & Techniques* (Washington, D.C.: United States Institute of Peace, 1999).

Espinosa, Carlos, "La Negociación como Terapia: Memoria, Identidad y Honor Nacional en el Proceso de Paz Ecuador-Peru," in Adrián Bonilla (ed.), *Ecuador-Perú: Horizontes de la Negociación y el Conflicto* (Quito: FLACSO, 1999).

Figueiredo, Claudio Barbosa, Brazilian army general, coordinator of MOMEP. Interview with the authors, Rio de Janeiro, March 15, 2001.

———, "MOMEP: Una Mision Cumplida," *Revista de Fuerzas Armadas del Ecuador* (June 1999): 55–62.

Franko, Patrice, "Patterns of Military Procurement in Latin America: Implications for U.S. Regional Policy," in Gabriel Marcella and Richard Downes (eds.), *Security Cooperation in the Western Hemi-*

sphere: Resolving the Ecuador-Peru Conflict (Miami: North-South Center Press, 1998).

Gallardo, José, army general and former minister of defense of Ecuador. Interview with the authors, Quito, April 5, 2001.

Gallegos, Bertha García, "New Perspectives on Using Diplomacy for the Resolution of the Ecuador-Peru Conflict," in Gabriel Marcella and Richard Downes (eds.), *Security Cooperation in the Western Hemisphere: Resolving the Ecuador-Peru Conflict* (Miami: North-South Center Press, 1998).

Gallegos, Bertha Garcia, Edy Kaufman, Oscar Schiappa-Pietra, Saúl Sosnowski, *Ecuador y Perú: Estrategias para la Resolución del Conflicto* (College Park: Maryland Group, 1997).

Geldres, Jorge Lázaro, "El Alcance de la Comisión Binacional Peruano-Ecuatoriana Sobre Medidas de Fomento," in Sandra Namihas (ed.), *El Processo de Conversaciones para la Solución del Diferendo Peruano-Ecuatoriano* (Lima: Fondo Editorial de la Pontificia Universidad Católica del Perú, 2000).

Goertz, Gary, and Paul Diehl, "(Enduring) Rivalries," in Manus I. Midlarsky (ed.), *Handbook of War Studies II* (Ann Arbor: University of Michigan Press, 2000).

———, "Enduring Rivalries: Theoretical Constructs and Empirical Patterns," *International Studies Quarterly* 37 (1995): 147–172.

Griffith, Ivelaw, "Security Collaboration and Confidence Building in the Americas," in Jorge I. Dominguez (ed.), *International Security & Democracy: Latin America and the Caribbean in the Post–Cold War Era* (Pittsburgh: University of Pittsburgh Press, 1998).

"The Guarantor Presidents' Letter, October 23, 1998," in Gabriel Marcella and Richard Downes (eds), *Security Cooperation in the Western Hemisphere: Resolving the Ecuador-Peru Conflict* (Miami: North-South Center Press), p. 246.

Hernandez, Luis, *La Guerra del Cenepa: Diario de un Comandante* (Quito: Corporacion Editora Nacional, 2000).

———, colonel of the Ecuadorian army, commander of the tactical group Iturralde. Interview with the authors, Quito, April 6, 2001.

Herz, Monica, "Brazilian Perspectives on the Redefinition of the Concept of Security." Paper presented at the ACUNS Twelfth Annual Meeting, New York, United Nations, 1999.

Hey, Jeanne, "Ecuadorian Foreign Policy Since 1979: Ideological Cycles or a Trend Toward Neoliberalism?" *Journal of Interamerican Studies and World Affairs* 37, 4 (1995): 57–73.

Holsti, K. J., *The State, War and the State of War* (Cambridge: Cambridge University Press, 1996).

Huerta, Francisco, member of the Ecuadorian delegation to the Commission on Confidence Building Measures. Interview with the authors, Quito, April 5, 2001.

"Itamaraty Peace Declaration Between Peru and Ecuador," February 17, 1995. *Resenha de Política Exterior do Brasil,* no. 76 (1995): 299–300.

Izaguirre, Carlos Reyna, "Diplomacia Presidencial y Mediatización de la Política," in Adrián Bonilla (ed.), *Ecuador-Perú: Horizontes de la Negociación y el Conflicto* (Quito: FLACSO, 1999).

Jackson, Robert H., *Quasi-States: Sovereignty, International Relations and the Third World* (Cambridge: Cambridge University Press, 1990).

Jepperson, Ronald L., Alexander Wendt, and Peter J. Katzenstein, "Norms, Identity, and Culture in National Security," in Peter Katzenstein (ed.), *The Culture of National Security* (New York: Columbia University Press, 1996).

Kay, Bruce H., "'Fujipopulism' and the Liberal State in Peru, 1990–1995," *Journal of Interamerican Studies and World Affairs* 38, 4 (1996): 55–98.

Klarén, Peter Flindell, *Peru: Society and Nationhood in the Andes* (New York: Oxford University Press, 2000).

Lafer, Celso, and Gelson Fonseca Jr., "Questões para a Diplomacia no Contexto Internacional das Polaridades Indefinidas (Notas Analíticas e Algumas Sugestões)," in Gélson Fonseca Júnior and Sérgio Henrique Nabuco de Castro (eds.), *Temas de Política Externa Brasileira II* (Rio de Janeiro: Paz e Terra, 1994).

Lampreia, Luis Felipe, Brazilian foreign minister during the mediation process. Interview with the authors, Rio de Janeiro, February 14, 2001.

Marcella, Gabriel, and Richard Downes, "The Ecuador-Peru Dispute and Conflict Resolution in the Americas," in Gabriel Marcella and Richard Downes (eds.), *Security Cooperation in the Western Hemisphere: Resolving the Ecuador-Peru Conflict* (Miami: North-South Center Press, 1999).

———, "Introduction," in Gabriel Marcella and Richard Downes (eds.), *Security Cooperation in the Western Hemisphere: Resolving the Ecuador-Peru Conflict* (Miami: North-South Center Press, 1999).

Mares, David R., *Violent Peace: Militarised Interstate Bargaining in Latin America* (New York: Columbia University Press, 2001).

Mares, David R., and Steven A. Bernstein, "The Use of Force in Latin American Interstate Relations," in Jorge I. Dominguez (ed.), *International Security & Democracy: Latin America and the Caribbean in the Post–Cold War Era* (Pittsburgh: University of Pittsburgh Press, 1998).

Mariz, Vasco, former Brazilian ambassador to Peru and Ecuador. Interview with the authors, Rio de Janeiro, February 12, 2001.

———, "O Brasil e o Conflito Peruano-Equatoriano," *Carta Mensal* 45 (Junho 1999): 41–58.

Martz, John D., "Studying Politics and the State in Ecuador," *Latin American Research Review* 32, 2 (1997): 170–183.

Maryland Group, *Ecuador-Perú: Hacia una Iniciativa Democrática y Cooperativa de Resolución de Conflitos* (University of Maryland, Maryland Group, 1997).

Merrills, J. G., *International Dispute Settlement* (Cambridge: Cambridge University Press, 1998).

Moncayo, Paco, General, former chief of staff of the Ecuadorian army. Interview with the authors, Quito, April 5, 2001.

"Montevideo Declaration," February 28, 1995. *Resenha de Política Exterior do Brasil,* no. 76 (1995): 302.

Moura, Gerson, "A Segurança Coletiva Continental: O Sistema Interamericano, O TIAR e a Guerra Fria," in José Guilhon de Alburquerque (ed.), *Sessenta Años de Política Externa Brasileira,* vol. 1 (São Paulo: Cultura Editores Associados, 1996).

Murphy, Alexander B., "The Sovereign State System as Political-Territorial Ideal: Historical and Contemporary Considerations," in T. J. Biersteker and C. Weber (eds.), *State Sovereignty as Social Construct* (Cambridge: Cambridge University Press, 1996).

Namihas, Sandra (ed.), *El Proceso de Conversaciones para la Solución del Diferendo Peruano-Ecuatoriano* (Lima: Fondo Editorial de la Pontificia Universidad Católica del Perú, 2000).

Nascimento, Antonio Carlos do, *Peru-Equador: Futuro de Paz/Perspectiva de Conflito, XXXIV Curso de Altos Estudos* (Brasilia: Foreign Relations Ministry–Rio Branco Institute, 1997).

Nolan, Janee E. (ed.), *Global Engagement Co-operation and Security in the 21st Century* (Washington, D.C.: Brookings Institution, 1994).

Novak, Fabián, legal adviser to the Peruvian delegation to the Commission on Border Demarcation. Interview with the authors, Lima, April 2, 2001.

Obando, Enrique, "Perú y los Procesos de Verificación," in Francisco Rojas Aravena (ed.), *Medidas de Confianza Mutua: Verificacion* (Santiago: FLACSO, 1996).

Palmer, David Scott, "Missed Opportunities and Misplaced Nationalism: Continuing Challenges to Multilateral Peacekeeping Efforts in the Peru-Ecuador Border Conflict," in Tommie Sue Montgomer (ed.), *Peacemaking and Democratization in the Western Hemisphere* (Miami: North-South Center, University of Miami, 2000).

———, "Peru-Ecuador Border Conflict: Missed Opportunities, Misplaced Nationalism, and Multilateral Peacekeeping," *Journal of Interamerican Studies & World Affairs* 39, 3 (1997): 109–148.

———, "The Search for Conflict Resolution: The Guarantors and the Peace Process in the Ecuador-Peru Dispute," in Gabriel Marcella and Richard Downes (eds.), *Security Cooperation in the Western Hemisphere: Resolving the Ecuador-Peru Conflic* (Miami: North-South Center Press, 1999).

"Peace Declaration of Itamaraty, February 17, 1995," in Gabriel Marcella and Richard Downes (eds.), *Security Cooperation in the Western Hemisphere: Resolving the Ecuador-Peru Conflict* (Miami: North-South Center Press), p. 242.

Permanent Council of the Organization of American States, Special Committee on Hemisphere Security, *Support for a New Concept of Hemisphere Security: Cooperative Security,* OEA/Ser.G,GE/SH-12/93 rev. 1. May 17, 1993.

"Presidential Act of Brasilia, October 26, 1998," in Gabriel Marcella and Richard Downes (eds.), *Security Cooperation in the Western Hemisphere: Resolving the Ecuador-Peru Conflict* (Miami: North-South Center Press), p. 244.

"Programas del Plan Binacional de Desarrollo de la Region Fronteriza," *Analisis Internacional*, no. 15 (Lima: CEPEI, 1998), pp. 326–293.

"Proposta dos Países Garantes para a Solução dos Desacordos, November 23, 1998," in Marcel Biato, *O Processo de Paz Equador-Peru e a Solução Pacífica de Controvérsias* (Brasília: Instituto Rio Branco–LVI Curso de Altos Estudos, 2001), pp. 245–246.

"Propuesta Integral Presentada por el Presidente de la Republica del Peru Ingeniero Alberto Fujimori, al Presidente de La Republica del Ecuador Doctor Rodrigo Borja, para Proceder a Culminar el Proceso Demarcatorio en los Tramos Pendientes de la Frontera, Asegurar el Libre Acceso a la Navegacion en el Rio Amazonas y Sus Afluentes Septentrionales y Obtener Acuerdos Permanetes de Integracion Fronteriza y Fomentar las Medidas de Confianza Mutua y Seguridade," January 10 (Lima: Ministry of Foreign Relations Peru, 1992).

"Protocol of Peace, Friendship and Borders Between Peru and Ecuador, February 14, 1942," in Gabriel Marcella and Richard Downes (eds.), *Security Cooperation in the Western Hemisphere: Resolving the Ecuador-Peru Conflict* (Miami: North-South Center Press), p. 239.

Radcliffe, Sarah, and Sallie Westwood, *Remaking the Nation: Place, Identity and Politics in Latin America* (London: Routledge, 1996).

"Reflections for Conversations Between Ecuador and Peru to Take Place in Brasília, November 1997," in Marcel Biato, *O Processo de Paz Equador-Peru e a Solução Pacífica de Controvérsias* (Brasília: Instituto Rio Branco–LVI Curso de Altos Estudos, 2001), pp. 252–253.

Rezek, Francisco, *Direito dos Tratados* (Rio de Janeiro: Editorial Forense, 1984).

Ribadeneira, Jose Mighel Vásconeza, "Del Protocolo de Rio de Janeiro a la Declaración Presidencial de Brasilia." Master's thesis, University of Brasilia, History Department, 2000.

Rizzo, Oliveira Eliézer, "Brazilian Diplomacy and the 1995 Ecuador-Peru War," in Gabriel Marcella and Richard Downes (eds.), *Security Cooperation in the Western Hemisphere: Resolving the Ecuador-Peru Conflict* (Miami: North-South Center Press, 1999).

"Santiago Accord, October 29, 1996," in Marcel Biato, *O Processo de Paz Equador-Peru e a Solução Pacífica de Controvérsias* (Brasília: Instituto Rio Branco–LVI Curso de Altos Estudos, 2001), p. 258.

Schereber, Efraín F., "La Declaración de Paz de Itamaraty," in Sandra Namihas (ed.), *El Processo de Conversaciones para la Solución del Diferendo Peruano-Ecuatoriano* (Lima: Fondo Editorial de la Pontificia Universidad Católica del Perú, 2000).

Schofi, Osmar, Brazilian ambassador to Ecuador between 1994 and 1999. Interview with the authors, Brasilia, April 4, 2001.

Shaw, Malcom N., *International Law* (Cambridge: Cambridge University Press, 2000).

Simas, Fernando, head of the Division for South America at the Brazilian Foreign Ministry. Interview with the authors, Brasilia, April 4, 2001.

Soares, João Baena, former secretary-general of the OAS. Interview with the authors, Rio de Janeiro, February 14, 2001.

Special Committee on Hemisphere Security, "Support for a New Concept of Hemisphere Security: Co-operative Security," OEA/Ser.G,GE/SH-12/93 rev. 1, May, 17, 1993.

St. John, Ronald Bruce, "The Boundary Between Ecuador and Peru," *Boundary and Territory Briefing* 1, 4 (1994): 1–20.

———, "Las Relaciones Ecuador y Perú: Una Perspectiva Histórica," in Adrián Bonilla (ed.), *Ecuador-Perú: Horizontes de la Negociación y el Conflicto* (Quito: FLACSO, 1999).

Susskind, Lawrence, and Eileen Babbitt, "Overcoming the Obstacles to Effective Mediation of International Disputes," in S. Touval and I. W. Zartman (eds.), *International Mediation in Theory and Practice* (Boulder: Westview Press, 1985).

Téran, Edgar, presiding over the Ecuadorian delegation and the delegation to the commission on trade and navigation. Interview with the authors, Quito, April 6, 2001.

"Tratado de Comércio y Navegacion Entre los Goviernos de la Republica del Peru y la Republica del Ecuador," *Analisis Internacional,* no. 15 (Lima: CEPEI, 1998), pp. 328–332.

Trazegnies, Fernando, former minister of foreign relations of Peru. Interview with the authors, Lima, April 2, 2001.

Uranga, Ruan Jose, Argentine representative to the negotiations. Interview with the authors, Brasilia, April 4, 2001.

Van Breugel-Douglas, Francisco Tudela, former minister of foreign affairs of Peru. Interview with the authors, Lima, April 3, 2001.

———, "Una Estrategia para la Paz," in Sandra Namihas (ed.), *El Proceso de Conversaciones para la Solución del Diferendo Peruano-Ecuatoriano* (Lima: Fondo Editorial de la Pontificia Universidad Católica del Perú, 2000).

Varas, Augusto, "Co-operative Hemispheric Security After the Cold War," in Olga Pellicer, *Regional Mechanisms and International Security in Latin America* (Tokyo: United Nations University, 1998).

Vasquez, John, "Distinguishing Rivals That Go to War from Those That Do Not: A Quantitative Comparative Case Study of the Two Paths to War," *International Studies Quarterly* 40 (1996): 531–558.

———, "Reexamining the Steps to War: New Evidence and Theoretical Insights," in Manus I. Midlarsky (ed.), *Handbook of War Studies II* (Ann Arbor: University of Michigan Press, 2000).

———, *The War Puzzle* (New York: Cambridge University Press, 1993).

Verde-Oliva, special edition (Brasília: Brazilian Army, 1999), n. 166.

Vivando, Eduardo Ponce, deputy foreign minister of Peru. Interview with the authors, Brasilia, April 4, 2001.

Wagner, Drago Kisic, "Acuerdo Amplio de Integración Fronteriza, Desarrollo y Vecindad: Estrategia y Negociación," in Sandra Namihas (ed.), *El Processo de Conversaciones para la Solución del Diferendo Peruano-Ecuatoriano* (Lima: Fondo Editorial de la Pontificia Universidad Católica del Perú, 2000).

Weidner, Glenn R, "Peacekeeping in the Upper Cenepa Valley: A Regional Response to Crisis," in Gabriel Marcella and Richard Downes (eds.), *Security Cooperation in the Western Hemisphere: Resolving the Ecuador-Peru Conflict* (Miami: North-South Center Press, 1999).

Wendt, Alexander, *Social Theory of International Politics* (Cambridge: Cambridge University Press, 1999).

Index

Act of Lima (1936), 32
Acuerdo de Distension ("gentlemen's agreement"), 41, 42
Aguas, Luis, 47
Amazon Basin conflict, 26–27, 29–30, 34, 35, 49, 54, 55, 56–57, 58, 59
American Declaration on the Rights and Duties of Man, 65
Andean Pact, 42, 74, 75
Argentina: as guarantor country, 7, 31–32, 34; Brazil's relations with, 70

Ballen, Duran, 46
Base Norte operation, 43–44, 45–46
Battle of Ayacucho, 25
Beagle Channel crisis of 1979, 42
Bilateral Commission on Confidence Building Measures, 59
Bolivar, Simon, 23
Border Demarcation Agreement, 59, 61
Border disputes, policy recommendations for, 102–103. *See also* Ecuador-Peru territorial disputes
Border Integration Accord, 59, 60–61
Borja, Rodrigo, 42
Brasilia Accords, 14, 17, 22, 47, 55, 61, 98, 100; access and rights of sovereignty in, 59–60; demarcation process and, 59; implementation of, 100; support for, 8
Brazil: and Amazon River Basin sover-

eignty, 70–71; as mediator and guarantor country, 7, 31–32, 34, 40–41; regional security role of, 70
Buenos Aires Conference, 65, 66

Calvo doctrine, 66
Canabrava, Ivan, 15, 54
Cardoso, Fernando Henrique, 7, 15, 59
Cartagena Declaration on Security and Cooperation, 42
Cédula Real royal decree, 26
Cenepa War, 13, 16, 21, 35, 43–47; casualties of, 47; and Ecuador's foreign policy, 46; Fujimori's re-election and, 76; guarantor countries' involvement in, 46, 47; 1991 crisis and, 39, 40–45; peace negotiations and resolution of, 46–47; Rio Protocol and, 22
Central American security environment, 67–68
Chapultepec Conference, 65
Chile, as guarantor country, 7
Civil society: and conflict resolution, 15, 87, 101–102
Clinton, Bill, 59
Conflict resolution: ad hoc instruments of, 102–103; bilateral and global interdependence and, 101; informal mechanisms of, 99–100; as mediation goal, 101; and military confrontation, 101; norm of peaceful resolution in, 99; as redefinition of

About This Publication

Although the 1995 Cenepa War between Ecuador and Peru was the first military conflict in South America in more than five decades, the Ecuador-Peru relationship might be characterized as one of enduring rivalry—punctuated by the threat of armed combat. In the context of this history of recurrent crises, Herz and Nogueira analyze the mediation process that followed the 1995 war.

The authors first consider the place that the ongoing rivalry occupied in the construction of the national identity of each country; they then explore the reasons that the 1995–1998 mediation process succeeded. The most significant factor in that success, they argue, was increasingly engaged mediators who worked to ensure that not only the objective but also the subjective aspects of the conflict were addressed to the satisfaction of both parties. Stressing that the strategies employed allowed for (and encouraged) the redefinition of identities and interests, they discuss the significance of the mediation process for the present Latin American security environment.

Monica Herz is lecturer and coordinator of the Graduate Program at the Catholic University of Rio de Janeiro's Institute of International Relations (IRI). **João Pontes Nogueira** is assistant professor of international politics at IRI.

The International Peace Academy

The International Peace Academy (IPA) is an independent, international institution dedicated to promoting the prevention and settlement of armed conflicts between and within states through policy research and development.

Founded in 1970, the IPA has built an extensive portfolio of activities in fulfillment of its mission:

- Symposiums, workshops, and other forums that facilitate strategic thinking, policy development, and organizational innovation within international organizations.
- Policy research on multilateral efforts to prevent, mitigate, or rebuild after armed conflict.
- Research, consultations, and technical assistance to support capacities for peacemaking, peacekeeping, and peacebuilding in Africa.
- Professional-development seminars for political, development, military, humanitarian, and nongovernmental personnel involved in peacekeeping and conflict resolution.
- Facilitation in conflict situations where its experience, credibility, and independence can complement official peace efforts.
- Outreach to build public awareness on issues related to peace and security, multilateralism, and the United Nations.

The IPA works closely with the United Nations, regional and other international organizations, governments, and nongovernmental organizations, as well as with parties to conflicts in selected cases. Its efforts are enhanced by its ability to draw on a worldwide network of government and business leaders, scholars, diplomats, military officers, and leaders of civil society.

The IPA is a nonprofit organization governed by an international Board of Directors. The organization is funded by generous donations from governments, major philanthropic foundations, and corporate donors, as well as contributions from individuals and its Board members.

International Peace Academy Publications

Available from Lynne Rienner Publishers, 1800 30th Street, Boulder, Colorado 80301 (303-444-6684), www.rienner.com.

Ending Civil Wars: The Implementation of Peace Agreements, edited by Stephen John Stedman, Donald Rothchild, and Elizabeth M. Cousens (2002)

Sanctions and the Search for Security: Challenges to UN Action, David Cortright and George A. Lopez, with Linda Gerber (2002)

Ecuador vs. Peru: Peacemaking Amid Rivalry, Monica Herz and João Pontes Nogueira (2002)

Liberia's Civil War: Nigeria, ECOMOG, and Regional Security in West Africa, Adekeye Adebajo (2002)

Building Peace in West Africa: Liberia, Sierra Leone, and Guinea-Bissau, Adekeye Adebajo (2002)

Kosovo: An Unfinished Peace, William G. O'Neill (2002)

From Reaction to Conflict Prevention: Opportunities for the UN System, edited by Fen Osler Hampson and David M. Malone (2002)

Peacemaking in Rwanda: The Dynamics of Failure, Bruce D. Jones (2001)

Self-Determination in East Timor: The United Nations, the Ballot, and International Intervention, Ian Martin (2001)

Civilians in War, edited by Simon Chesterman (2001)

Toward Peace in Bosnia: Implementing the Dayton Accords, Elizabeth M. Cousens and Charles K. Cater (2001)

Sierra Leone: Diamonds and the Struggle for Democracy, John L. Hirsch (2001)

Peacebuilding as Politics: Cultivating Peace in Fragile Societies, edited by Elizabeth M. Cousens and Chetan Kumar (2001)

The Sanctions Decade: Assessing UN Strategies in the 1990s, David
Cortright and George A. Lopez (2000)
Greed and Grievance: Economic Agendas in Civil War, edited by Mats
Berdal and David M. Malone (2000)
Building Peace in Haiti, Chetan Kumar (1998)
Rights and Reconciliation: UN Strategies in El Salvador, Ian Johnstone
(1995)